40 Days to a Prosperous Soul

DESTINY IMAGE BOOKS BY DR. CINDY TRIMM

The 40 Day Soul Fast

40 Days to Discovering the Real You

Reclaim Your Soul

40 Days to Reclaiming Your Soul

The Prosperous Soul

PUSH

Prevail

Heal Your Soul, Heal the World
(Coming Soon!)

40 Days to a
Prosperous Soul

*Your Interactive Guide
to Living a Richer Life*

CINDY TRIMM

DESTINY IMAGE® PUBLISHERS, INC.

P.O. Box 310, Shippensburg, PA 17257-0310

"Promoting Inspired Lives."

This book and all other Destiny Image and Destiny Image Fiction books are available at Christian bookstores and distributors worldwide.

Cover design by Eileen Rockwell

For more information on foreign distributors, call 717-532-3040.

Reach us on the Internet: www.destinyimage.com.

ISBN 13 TP: 978-0-7684-0522-4

ISBN 13 Ebook: 978-0-7684-0523-1

For Worldwide Distribution, Printed in the U.S.A.

1 2 3 4 5 6 7 8 / 19 18 17 16 15

*Beloved, I pray that you may prosper in all things
and be in health, just as your soul prospers.*
—JOHN[1]

*I came so they can have real and eternal life, more
and better life than they ever dreamed of.*
—JESUS[2]

---

1   3 John 1:2
2   John 10:10 MSG

CONTENTS

INTRODUCTION

This devotional is designed to be your daily companion on this 40-day journey to experiencing a richer life. The goal of the *Prosperous Soul* message is different from the previous two books. Here, we are not focusing on what we are moving away from, but rather what we are pressing toward. After reading *The 40 Day Soul Fast* and *Reclaim Your Soul*, it is time for you to catch a glimpse of God's divine blueprint for a truly prosperous soul. Once you are living authentically and walking in freedom, it is time for you to take the next step—the pursuit of wholeness.

This book and devotional is your "Now what" plan for soul freedom. Isn't this often the question that we ask? From coming to Christ for the first time to experiencing a life-changing deliverance or healing, the experience is always followed up by, "Now what?" In other words, *"How do I live from this place of freedom? How do I sustain authenticity? How do I experience fullness, wholeness, and abundance in every area of my life?"* Jesus always meant for our spiritual experiences with Him to be gateways into new realms of living. Whether you gave your life to Christ at the church altar, on the street, or kneeling by your bed, these 40 daily practices for prospering your soul will keep you living in abundance every single day.

This is your *how-to* guide for your next season, and I am believing that your next season is going to be abundant in every way!

With this in mind, I encourage you to walk out your journey with those you relate with most. Select two or three others as your circle-of-trust companions. These individuals will become your accountability support team. You might also recommend this tool to your book club or choose to journey with a larger group. This daily devotional can be especially useful as a field guide for a small group study—or as a resource to strengthen your most intimate relationships. Let this be a journey of true prosperity and wholeness for everyone closest to you.

There is nothing more wonderful than living a prosperous life. This is what Jesus came to give you. Yet for too long, we have defined prosperity in a narrow, one-dimensional manner. It is not merely the acquisition of wealth, but it is enjoying richness in every area of life as you are equipped and empowered to overcome obstacles, grow through personal crises, and surmount life challenges beginning with prospering your soul.

How to Use the Devotional with the Book

Each day in this devotional matches the corresponding day found in Part Two of *The Prosperous Soul* book. The daily devotional is designed to help you implement the 40 daily practices that are taught in the book. You will occasionally see some crossover from the book, but the vast majority of what you will interact with in the pages to come is action driven. In other words, I want to give you tools and strategies for taking the concepts you learned about in *The Prosperous Soul* and putting them to work in your everyday life. The book provided the concept; The devotional will help you effectively apply the principles and implement the strategies.

To take full advantage of this 40-day study, you should read each day's chapter in the book, and then follow up with the reading and activities found in the devotional. The questions, exercises, and activation prayers are designed to help you take what you've learned in the book and proactively apply it to your life. Gaining information only increases your bank of head knowledge *unless* you put hands and feet to it; then it becomes transformation—and that is where you are going with this journey.

I would encourage you to take 30 minutes out of your day to read the chapter in the book and then work through the meditations and exercises outlined in the devotional. You can also break up your study by reading the chapter at one point in the day and revisiting the devotional at another. It is important that you use this devotional with the book to get the most out of your experience.

Here is how the devotional is divided up:

DAILY PRACTICE

This devotional insight simply reminds you of what the daily practice is, why it is important to your soul's prosperity, and how you can start implementing it in your daily life. It will be the same for both the book and for the devotional. These are the key practices or habits essential to living a richer life.

REFLECTION QUESTIONS

This devotional/journal is designed to be interactive. As you progress through the exercises over the next 40 days, write down your thoughts and insights and record your feelings. These questions are designed to get you thinking about and interacting with the material you read in both the book and devotional. When you are able to wrap your mind around where you stand in relation to each practice, you will be well on your way to effectively incorporating them into your daily life. Remember, the devotional is yours. Make it personal. Complete transparency will allow the Holy Spirit to take your soul on a journey of freedom, healing, and empowerment. There are no right or wrong responses.

ACTION STEPS

Putting the disciplines into practice so that they become habits that turn into a lifestyle is the purpose of this journey. These action steps help you practically put into action what you've been learning and thinking about each day. They are not random. Rather, they are simple tools purposed to help you step out on what you are discovering and make progressive steps toward living out the daily practice you've just studied.

Putting the disciplines into practice so that they become habits that turn into a lifestyle is the purpose of this journey.

Week One

SPIRITUAL PROSPERITY

*No pessimist ever discovered the secret of the
stars, or sailed to an uncharted land, or opened
a new doorway for the human spirit.*
—HELEN KELLER

Day One

GOD'S WORD

The Word we study has to be the Word we pray. My personal experience of the relentless tenderness of God came not from exegetes, theologians, and spiritual writers, but from sitting still in the presence of the living Word and beseeching Him to help me understand with my head and heart His written Word. Sheer scholarship alone cannot reveal to us the gospel of grace.
—BRENNAN MANNING
The Ragamuffin Gospel[1]

God's Word is our foundational blueprint for experiencing the prosperous life. The key is measuring true prosperity by God's definition of the concept, not the world's. Remember, it is in no way limited to the mere acquisition of material wealth or gain. This is only one expression of prosperity. We will experience a true, holistic definition when we give ourselves to studying the Scripture, for God's Word unveils what true prosperity looks like.

Being in God's Word is an essential practice to experiencing prosperity. Yet, at the same time, we cannot go into the Bible with a religious agenda and read into it—using our preconceived ideas and opinions as a filter for understanding what God is conveying. In other words, we do not engage God's Word because of what it does for God. It does not impact Him one way or the other. It does not increase or decrease God's love toward you. His affection is set and unchanging. He loves you whether you are in the Word or out of the Word. However, you become more *aware* of His love toward you when you make God's Word your top priority. In addition, you become aware of every promise that He has made available. *This* is living in true spiritual prosperity—accessing every promise and blessing that God has made readily available to you. The problem is, many of us don't know what is available because we have not spent time reading His will—and it is His Word that unveils His will.

So I ask you, what is the place of the Word of God in your life? Do you give it the respect that you should? Do you read and study it regularly looking for insight into who God is and what He has planned for you? Do you read it in search of strategies for life and living? Do you focus on it attentively when you read it, or when it is read to you in a Bible study—or listen for the wisdom it imparts during a sermon so God can speak to you through it?

REFLECTION QUESTIONS

I want you to take this opportunity and evaluate your current level of engagement with God's Word. We've provided space to respond below. Please be honest. No one else is reading this *except for you.*

How much time do you spend in the Word? (Is it daily, weekly, monthly, or hardly at all?)

What is this process currently like for you? (Is it boring? A struggle? Or joyful and exciting?)

Do you experience difficulty understanding the Bible translation that you are currently reading?

What are your motives in reading God's Word? (Are you reading it for your benefit, or do you think that if you read more of the Bible, you gain more favor with God?)

ACTION STEPS

*Your word is a lamp to guide my feet
and a light for my path.*
PSALM 119:105 NLT

1. *Find a translation of the Bible that is easy for you to read and understandable.* A study Bible is always a good place to start (we recommend the English Standard Version, the New King James Version, or the New International Version for your primary text; the New Living Translation and the Message Bible are great resources to provide a more contemporary reading of the text; and finally, if you are looking to go deeper into a particular word, phrase, or concept, the Amplified Bible or Dake's Bible are great additional tools to have on hand.)

2. *Begin a daily plan that works for you.* It is important for you to read the Word of God on a daily basis. This is a key spiritual discipline that, ultimately, positions you to experience the prosperous life that God, your heavenly Father, has made available to all of His children. Too many Christians live beneath their Kingdom rights and privileges, not because God is unwilling to bless them, but because they simply remain ignorant to what they possess in Christ and of their inheritance. The Word reveals what belongs to you, and the Holy Spirit is the One who helps you understand the Scriptures clearly so you can discern every blessing and benefit God has made freely available to you.

3. *Start with small steps.* Quantity is not what matters most; it's quality. If you are able to give five focused minutes to the Word of God daily, go into that time without the distractions of TV, cell phones, or social media, and ask the Holy Spirit to make it enriching for you. He knows your schedule. We cannot be religious about it. So many have dismissed and ditched their daily routine of reading the Bible because they have placed

unreasonable expectations upon themselves. Reading God's Word is a blessing, not a burden.

4. *Begin a one-year Bible program.* This is one option, but certainly not the only option. There are plenty of free resources available online for this, as well as the actual *One Year Bible* to help guide you through the journey.

5. *Don't just open up the Bible and start reading randomly.* Some have attempted to do this and, unfortunately, opened to books like Leviticus or Deuteronomy. These are challenging places for anyone to begin in developing a habit of daily Bible reading. It is *not* more spiritual to read the Bible all the way through from Genesis to Revelation. It is a great plan, but it is not the only one. I recommend looking up topics of interest in the concordance and studying those. There might be certain biblical characters who intrigue you or stories you would like to explore. Perhaps you are reading through a particular book or devotional. Take a key Scripture the author provides and study it in more depth. Truly, the sky is the limit when it comes to *how* you approach God's Word. The most important thing is that you make His Word a daily priority.

1. Brennan Manning, *The Ragamuffin Gospel* (Sisters, OR: Multnomah Publishers, 2000), 45.

Day Two

PRAYER

*Don't fret or worry. Instead of worrying, pray.
Let petitions and praises shape your worries into
prayers, letting God know your concerns. Before
you know it, a sense of God's wholeness, everything
coming together for good, will come and settle you
down. It's wonderful what happens when Christ
displaces worry at the center of your life.*
—PHILIPPIANS 4:6-7 MSG

f anyone dealt with circumstances, trials, and opposition in life, it was the apostle Paul. If you are going through a difficult season, you can probably relate to Paul in some way. Look at the passage found in Philippians 4:6-7, and consider the context in which the author was writing. Paul was persecuted. He was shipwrecked. He was beaten. He was taken to trial. Paul was left for dead. And yet, the same Paul who experienced all of those hardships encourages readers by telling them, *"Don't fret or worry."* How in the world was he able to do this? How could this man enjoy soul prosperity and abundance even in the midst of some hard-hitting circumstances and trials?

Philippians 4:6-7 gives us Paul's response and 1 Thessalonians 5:17 reveals his secret. How was it that Paul could walk in soul prosperity even during the difficult times? His secret was to *"pray continually"* (1 Thess. 5:17 NIV). The different translations of this one verse give greater insight into what it looks like to embrace a lifestyle of prayer.

- Never stop praying. (NLT)

- Pray without ceasing. (ESV)

- Pray constantly. (HCSB)

- Pray all the time. (MSG)

Certainly we should set aside specific times to pray; however, we cannot just do our "God time," cross prayer off our list, and then move on with our lives. Paul's secret to living in a place of spiritual prosperity was that prayer wasn't just a part of life; it *was* his life. He was constantly drawing from Heaven's divine resources because he lived in nonstop fellowship with God through prayer.

Of course, we should engage the practical side of having a daily prayer time (in the same way you would have daily time in the Word). Whether you keep a prayer journal, pray over a set of Scriptures, or read from a series of proclamations or declarations, taking just fifteen minutes every morning to acknowledge who is first in your life will transform your day. It also sets the tone of your day. Just be sure to posture your heart correctly in prayer, not simply to punch your spiritual timecard—but open your ears to hear what the Creator of the Universe wants to say to you throughout the day. His desire is for continuous conversation and dialogue—and oftentimes, at the most random moments! God is always speaking. The question is, *"Are you always listening?"* Living in this dimension of prayer begins with the expectation that God *wants* to talk to you on a regular basis.

Paul lived in a place of abundance and prosperity because he lived with ears constantly tuned in to Heaven's frequency. He understood that prayer was not simply laying out requests before God and then going about the day (although we should take time to present our requests to the Lord). Rather, Paul saw prayer as a *dialogue,* where we take as much time to listen as we do to speak… even if God seems silent. I find that often He answers much more with His presence than He does with words—and in that presence over the years, I have found more answers than I ever imagined possible as the Spirit of God planted His thoughts into the seed-bed of my mind.

REFLECTION QUESTIONS

What is your prayer life currently like? What would you like to see changed?

_____

_____

_____

_____

_____

What do you think it means to *pray continually?*

_____

_____

_____

_____

Have you experienced God answering you with His presence? What did this look like?

_____

_____

ACTION STEPS

*Prayer...is an art which only the Holy Spirit can teach
us. Pray for prayer. Pray until you can really pray.*
—CHARLES H. SPURGEON

Change the way you approach prayer today! Take time to come before the Lord, but ask Him to keep the conversation going. Posture your heart before the Holy Spirit, expecting to hear His voice throughout the day. Remember, this was one of Paul's secrets to living in a place of prosperity and abundance, even in the midst of some extraordinary difficulties.

I encourage you to approach the Lord in the morning and ask Him to help you engage this new dimension of dialogue-based prayer. Take this journal with you and write down how the Holy Spirit speaks to you throughout the day. His voice may come in subtle impressions. He may specifically direct you to pray for someone or a unique situation. Simply open your heart and open your ears to the God who desires communication with His people!

MEDITATION

*Such as are your habitual thoughts, such also
will be the character of your mind; for the soul
becomes dyed with the color of its thoughts.*
—MARCUS AURELIUS
Meditations

*B*iblical meditation is not emptying the mind; it is filling it with truth. It is maintaining a fixed mental focus on what the Word of God says. It is reorienting our thought life to come into agreement with the very thoughts of God. When it comes to meditation, it is important for us to get practical, otherwise it is easy to over-spiritualize the process.

Our thoughts need to represent the character of Christ. In fact, you can begin the meditation process right now! Consider these truths:

1. The mind of Christ has been given to you. "*We have the mind of Christ*" (1 Cor. 2:16 KJV).

2. Having His mind, you can think His thoughts. "*Have this mind among yourselves, which is yours in Christ Jesus*" (Phil. 2:5 ESV).

3. You can continually keep your mind set on higher things. "*And set your minds and keep them set on what is above (the higher things)*" (Col. 3:2 AMP).

Think on these scriptures for a moment. These three truths are worth meditating on because they reveal what you have access to *in Christ*. You can change the way you think. It is possible, like Marcus Aurelius wrote, that your soul can become "dyed" by *higher thoughts*—the thoughts of God. This is not New Age thinking; this is what Paul was writing about in Romans 12:2, where he described the process of renewing the mind.

Are you moving toward the prosperous soul that God wills for you—or are you meditating on things that move you away from the truth hidden in God's Word? You can know instantly by evaluating the nature of your thoughts. What thoughts do you allow to linger in your mind as you go about the business of living each day? Are you pressing God for greater insight and understanding? Are you asking big questions and meditating on His promises? Are you consumed with the problems in the world or the possibilities of His universe? Are you believing God for breakthrough ideas and innovations within your field of work, whether in the arts, science, entertainment, business, education, technology, medicine, government, media, social work, or ministry?

REFLECTION QUESTIONS

What does meditation look like to you? Have you had any past experience with meditation? If so, what was that like?

_____

_____

_____

_____

_____

If you have participated in eastern meditation, I encourage you to pause right now and renounce your involvement with those practices. Such is a counterfeit of how meditation functions in the Kingdom of God.

Pray:

> *Father, I renounce my involvement with eastern meditation (list, specifically, what kind of meditation you were involved in). I acknowledge this is a counterfeit of what You offer. I declare the blood of Jesus over my mind and thank You, Holy Spirit, that You have given me access to the thoughts of God. Fill my mind with those thoughts, Lord. And help me walk in the abundant life You have made available by helping me renew my mind according to Your Word. In Jesus's Name, Amen!*

Why do you think meditation on the Word of God is a link to living the abundant, prosperous life that God has made available to you?

_____

_____

_____

_____

_____

_____

ACTION STEPS

I meditate on your precepts and consider your ways.
PSALM 119:15 NIV

Begin to take small pieces of Scripture and start meditating upon them. Even though it is our tendency to want to read through sizable portions of the Bible to gain that sense of accomplishment, quality meditation is more important than a quantity of reading. This is why many people who read the Bible claim that they do not understand what they read immediately after reading it. Start to practice the art of biblical meditation. Even if you do read a larger portion of Scripture, select key verses that stood out to you and think about them. Write them out and record your reflections on what the Holy Spirit is speaking through the text. You will be amazed at how you can powerfully encounter God through the practice of meditation on the Scriptures.

Day Four

FASTING

When you fast...
—MATTHEW 6:16

I have heard people make the observation that Jesus specifically said, "*When* you fast..."—He did not say *if* you fast. This strongly suggests that Jesus was giving a glimpse of a spiritual practice that would become normative for believers throughout time immemorial. So, what does it mean to fast, and why is fasting so important?

In *The Prosperous Soul* book, I provide much more detail on the practice of fasting and also give some different examples of kinds of fasts that you can pursue. The importance of the fast is *not* the fast itself. Instead, it is the *focus* of the fast. Throughout the Old Testament, you see examples of people fasting, but their fasts produced nothing of significance in their lives and communities. Isaiah explained why in Isaiah 58. They engaged in the practice of fasting without drawing from the power of God. This is because their hearts were distant. The fast was nothing more than a religious front and a ritual. God does not want us going through fruitless motions. He gives us tools, such as fasting, to position us to live out the abundant, prosperous life that He has made available. There is always an "other side" to fasting—the results that it should produce in our lives.

In fact, true fasting is about alignment and produces action. Fasting aligns us with the plans, purposes, and power of Heaven and the fruit is a lifestyle that is further yielded to the Lord. *True fasting* changes our hearts and repositions us to live in greater devotion to God. It helps keep our focus singular—on the King and His Kingdom. When He comes into full view, we will see everything else in its proper perspective. Unfortunately, many of us are unable to maintain this "full view focus" on the Lord because of the many other voices and distractions that are pulling us every which way. This is not a call for escapism or radical detachment, as we have been assigned to the world *for the benefit of the world*. Unfortunately, we will not be of benefit to our sphere of influence if our focus is off. God is the Author of every solution that can bring life, healing, and wholeness to a hurting world. He is not only walking with us; He lives inside of us through the Holy Spirit. To live aware of this and then draw from His mighty power working within us is to maximize our potential to bless the world.

Again, fasting realigns our focus, helping us to keep our eyes fixed on the Author and Finisher of our faith, Christ Jesus. When He is at the center, everything else will come into its proper place—only then are we able to serve the world from a place of abundance, walking in the abundance of His grace.

REFLECTION QUESTIONS

What kind of experience have you had with fasting in the past?

_____

_____

_____

_____

_____

_____

Did you experience any significant results from the fast/fasts that you participated in? If so, what were they?

_____

_____

_____

_____

_____

If you did *not* experience any significant results from your fast, what do you think was the problem? (Evaluate your motives going into the fast.)

_____

_____

_____

_____

_____

ACTION STEPS

Fasting is the most powerful spiritual discipline of all the Christian disciplines. Through fasting and prayer, the Holy Spirit can transform your life.
—BILL BRIGHT

Try a fast this week! I am not telling you to fast 40 days or dive into an "all water" fast. In fact, I want to simply encourage you to take a day and try it out. Remember, it does not need to be a food fast either. The key is *replacement* and *alignment*. If we just give something up, but do not replace it with anything else, we are not fasting. Fasting is not simply about what we give up, but it is what we replace it with.

If you give up a meal, take the time you would ordinarily spend eating and spend it with God in prayer, worship, and the studying of God's Word. Likewise, if you give up something like social media or watching television for a day, be sure to replace those activities with practices that will enrich your spirit.

FELLOWSHIP

*Believers are not compared to bears or lions or other
animals that wander alone. Those who belong to
Christ are sheep in this respect, that they love to get
together. Sheep go in flocks, and so do God's people.*
—CHARLES H. SPURGEON

We are the body of Christ. In 1 Corinthians 12, the apostle Paul uses this language very intentionally in describing the community—or fellowship—of believers. A body is comprised of many different members, all working together to contribute to a highly functional unit. Jesus called this unit the Church in Matthew 16:18. For the Church to be the mighty force that Jesus envisioned, it needs to be operating in unity and in fellowship.

Consider the analogy that Paul draws from. As every member of our physical body works together, we are able to operate at maximum capacity. Likewise, when certain members of our body are not functioning, or worse, functioning in opposition to one another, we are restrained from efficiency and progress.

John Donne rightly acknowledged that, "No man is an island." As I described in the book, the community of believers has actually been called *"the fellowship of the mystery"* (Eph. 3:9). It is incredible to contemplate all that this means. When we gather together with other believers, we must elevate our thinking concerning what is actually taking place. It is not simply gathering in a sanctuary on Sunday or meeting together mid-week for a Bible study; it is not just coffee and movies and board games and potlucks.

Something happens in the spirit realm when men and women, boys and girls gather together in the presence of God who all carry within them the same Spirit. There is a multiplied dimension of anointing that is experienced and released. This is a mystery, because we all have equal access to God. The Holy Spirit has been given to every single believer and yes, as Martin Luther and the pioneers of the Protestant Reformation taught, every single Christian is in fact a "priest" before God.

That said, Peter did not use language to imply that God's priests (you and I) were to work alone. In 1 Peter 2:9, he explains, *"You are a chosen race, a royal priesthood, a holy nation, a people for his own possession, that you may proclaim the excellencies of him who called you out of darkness into his marvelous light"* (ESV). What do you notice about his language? It all implies community and person-to-person fellowship. We are a *chosen race*, a *royal priesthood*, a *holy nation*, a *people*. Yes, we are individuals, but we are also the sum of a whole—the body of Christ. True, we are powerful individually, but just imagine what happens when we come together in fellowship.

REFLECTION QUESTIONS

Why do you think living in fellowship with other believers is so important when it comes to accomplishing God's plans and purposes in the earth?

_____

What can fellowship accomplish that individualism cannot?

_____

How are you currently enjoying fellowship with other like-minded believers? Is this experience satisfying? If not, what are some ways that you could enrich your fellowship?

_____

ACTION STEPS

Change the way you view fellowship. This is the key action step you need to take if you are going to experience every blessing that God wants you to draw from being in fellowship with other believers. You cannot approach church as simply "going to church" and sitting in a building. Likewise, you must change the way you see other church-related activities. Remember, when the "fellowship of the mystery" assembles together, power is released. Iron sharpens iron. The weak are made strong. Gifts are activated. Destinies are realized. Potential is activated. *This* is how you should see fellowship.

Week Two

INTELLECTUAL PROSPERITY

*A man's mind may be likened to a garden, which
may be intelligently cultivated or allowed to run
wild; but whether cultivated or neglected, it must,
and will, bring forth. If no useful seeds are put into
it, then an abundance of useless weed seeds will fall
therein, and will continue to produce their kind.*
—JAMES ALLEN
As a Man Thinketh

Day Six

READING

Not all readers are leaders, but all leaders are readers.
—HARRY TRUMAN

*R*eading can do a lot of things for you. Just like stacking books one on top of another can literally help to extend your reach beyond your physical height, reading can help you grow to greater intellectual, social, financial, and spiritual heights; explore limitless destinations and places of interest; and extract wisdom from the minds of history's great thinkers, innovators, inventors, and leaders. Reading can help you solve problems, unveil mysteries, and develop new insights. It can give you an understanding of things that are not easily understood by non-readers.

Reading opens new, old, and even unopened doors of wisdom. Reading completely engages the mind. If you are looking to live a rich life intellectually, embark on a daily reading journey. Highly accomplished individuals all share one thing in common—they read. Reading elevates your mind; it exercises your brain and causes you to become a better, more effective thinker. Other forms of media do not place as high a demand on your mind to process concepts and ideas as does reading. Think about it. Movies, TV, and anything highly visual in nature delivers all of the images to you. When you read, your mind is forced to imagine the images. Your mind is the creative force in the process of reading.

Books have the ability to take you into great minds and pivotal times. They let you explore the decisions that were made, the mistakes, the triumphs, and the defeats, as well as the principles that were learned and lived. Reading lets you explore beyond the boundaries of what is accepted as possible and say, "Why not?" Books invite you to learn from the mistakes of others without having to make those same mistakes yourself. You can gain insight into the personalities and humanity of great men and women of God, or learn about your industry, history, politics, innovation, humanitarianism, or whatever other field piques your interest.

As author George R. R. Martin put it, "A reader lives a thousand lives before he dies.... The man who never reads lives only one." If you desire to experience new levels of intellectual abundance and prosperity, make reading a regular part of your everyday life!

REFLECTION QUESTIONS

Do you like reading? What would you say prevents you from reading more? Can you commit yourself to read, learn, and become a student again? Are you up for the challenge? Choose a book you've always meant to read and go buy it or check it out from the library—today!

If you were to develop a reading plan, what would it look like? Thirty minutes before bedtime, ten pages on your lunch hour? Write down some ideas for a doable daily routine below. Be creative. Remember, these exercises are not about giving you more "busywork" to do in life. They are dedicated to helping you cultivate daily practices to usher you into new levels of intellectual prosperity and richness.

ACTION STEPS

A book, too, can be a star, a living fire to lighten the darkness, leading out into the expanding universe.
—MADELEINE L'ENGLE

Now that you've had a moment to think about how an ideal reading plan would look, start to put it into practice. We will never reap the benefits of reading unless we read...even if only a little at a time.

Day Seven

FOCUS

*I've got my eye on the goal, where God is
beaconing us onward—to Jesus.*
—PHILIPPIANS 3:14 MSG

*I*t is important for us to keep our focus *fixed*. Once again, we return to the apostle Paul. If anyone lived with a sharp focus, it was this great forerunner of the Christian faith. His focus was undivided. He said "No" to lesser things in order to fully give his mind and attention to what was before him. Truly, he was intentional with his focus—a characteristic we would do well to model if we desire to prosper in our intellect and minds.

If you do not discover the power and potential of intentionality, distraction will consistently rob you of opportunity, creativity, and potentially your destiny. In *Reclaim Your Soul*, I reminded you that purpose is God's job; destiny is yours. God assigns you a purpose; however, you need to be a good steward of that purpose by positioning yourself in such a way that you will achieve the tasks at hand and thus fulfill your destiny. To fulfill your destiny, you must be focused.

I don't want it to sound like everything falls on you and that there is no divine aid involved. This is far from the truth. There is an amazing intersection that takes place when we, aware that God has assigned us a unique purpose, take the everyday steps to position ourselves for destiny-defining moments. In short,

God supernaturally blesses your focus. I cannot overestimate the power of a focused life in the hands of a supernatural God. Focus demonstrates your willingness to run faithfully with the purpose God has given you.

Distraction also robs us from focusing on what *God* is doing and how we can participate in His activity. Henry Blackaby, author of *Experiencing God*, has famously reminded us to always be on the lookout for where God is moving and what God is doing. This is our invitation to get involved. We don't ask God, "Bless what I am doing." Instead, we want to go where He is blessing. This demands focus. It demands eyes that are trained to see. God wants to use you mightily to accomplish His mighty purposes. One way we demonstrate our availability and usefulness is remaining focused on the tasks He gives us.

Being distracted by the common goings-on of everyday life will prevent you from tuning in to Heaven's frequency. We talked earlier about how God desires to engage you in a constant dialogue. He wants to release ideas, strategies, inventions, innovations, and other untapped expressions of creativity so that you can make a positive difference in your world.

The barrier? Smart phones with texts and emails. Social media with endless notifications and updates. Newsfeeds. Devices. We are plugged in on all fronts. The barrage of noise seems relentless. Technology is not bad in and of itself; it becomes destructive, however, when we do not know how to focus. Now, add to this all of the legitimate areas of focus—family, friends, your boss, your pets, your hobbies—and it is an absolute wonder if we ever get *anything* done.

It is time for you to get focused—give yourself wholeheartedly to whatever you are doing in the moment. "*Whatever your task, put yourselves into it, as done for the Lord*" (Col. 3:23 NRSV). Diligently put your whole self into whatever purpose you have been assigned. Most certainly, there will be multiple tasks and a variety of opportunities. The key is wholly devoting your focus to each one in its season so you can be a good steward of every blessed opportunity Heaven extends your way!

REFLECTION QUESTIONS

Do you feel like you consistently get things accomplished in your life? Yes _____ No _____

If "*no*," pause a moment and evaluate your level of focus. Describe the link between your level of accomplishment and your level of focus.

_____

_____

_____

_____

_____

If "*yes*," remember—you can always improve and experience increase! There are no limitations to the person who has resolved to live a focused life. What are some ways you can practically increase your level of focus in your job? Personal projects? Goals and dreams?

_____

_____

_____

_____

_____

_____

ACTION STEPS

Focusing is about saying "No."
—STEVE JOBS

One area we all need to grow in is the ability to say "no" to the lesser things and "yes" to the most important things. Life is a 24/7 balancing act. The first "yes" of our lives belongs to God. The next "yes" goes to our families, friends, and relationships. Everything else should follow those key areas.

Let me pose one final question: What things do you need to say "no" to in order to say "yes" to the more important things in life? When you say "no" to the wrong things, you are able to say "yes" to the right things.

Day Eight

CREATIVITY

*Then God said, "Let Us make man in Our
image, according to Our likeness...."*
—GENESIS 1:26

e reminded, you were made in the image and likeness of the Creator! I am convinced that there are unspeakable, unfathomable realms of creativity that God is waiting to release into the earth, but He is waiting for His people to represent Him in this way.

The earth is filled with needs that *you* carry possible solutions for. Those solutions are birthed in creativity. Many function in their created identity without even recognizing that this is how they were fashioned and wired. As those formed in God's own image, we are born with certain inherent creative tendencies. Now, just imagine what becomes possible to the man or woman who recognizes his/her place as a co-creator with the Creator of the Universe. We no longer strive to create apart from God; we create *with* Him, actively receiving His divine strategies and ideas. You are the vessel through whom God continues to create in the earth!

God continues to lead the way in creativity *through* people made in His image and likeness. He is *not* directly creating anything new in the earth realm. Consider all of the advancements and innovations that have been made in recent history. Medicine.

Technology. Space exploration. The list is endless. Who are the ones leading the way in these arenas of innovation? *People.*

Yes, God ultimately deserves all of the glory for these developments. He is the author of creativity, but humankind is the creative steward of God in the earth. What an opportunity we have been given! Even Mark Bryan, Julia Cameron, and Catherine Allen, the authors of *The Artist's Way at Work*, recognized this by writing, "Creativity...is not limited to a select few. It is a universal, not an elitist, gift.... Creativity belongs, as a birthright, to all of us."[1] Did you catch that last statement?

Creativity is your birthright.

It is not a question of whether or not you are a creative type. *You are.* The question is, *"Am I being a good steward of my creative nature?"* The key is cultivating your creativity on a daily basis. You need to develop it, just like you would your muscles through weight lifting.

You develop your creativity by paying attention to the world around you. You can discover keys to amazing breakthroughs by doing things that help you grow and prosper. Embrace creativity as part of your daily process—practicing and enhancing it however your heart is led. Play music, paint pictures, journal, blog, craft, bake, cook, experiment, tinker—take time to just let yourself imagine possibilities. The key is stepping out and releasing your creativity. If you let Him, the Spirit of God will lead you into incredible and marvelous things. He has manifold mysteries that He wants to share and help you unravel.

REFLECTION QUESTIONS

List some ways you consider yourself to be creative:

_____

_____

_____

_____

What are you currently doing to exercise your creativity on a daily/regular basis?

Are there areas in your life where you would like to focus your creativity more specifically? If so, what are they? (Or what would you like them to be?)

ACTION STEPS

Imagination is everything. It is the
preview of life's coming attractions.
—ALBERT EINSTEIN

Release your creative side! Ask yourself, *"Where do I consider myself creative?"* I don't care what your profession or personality is—you were made in the image of the Creator. There are creative tendencies wired into your very DNA. Remember, it's not *if* you are creative; it is *how* you are creative. Take a moment to do some journaling and ask the Holy Spirit to help you identify areas where you have creative tendencies.

_____

_____

_____

_____

_____

_____

_____

_____

_____

_____

_____

_____

_____

_____

_____

_____

_____

1. Mark Bryan with Julia Cameron and Catherine Allen, *The Artist's Way at Work: Twelve Weeks to Creative Freedom* (New York: William Morrow and Company, Inc., 1998), xix.

Day Nine

STUDY

*Study hard, for the well is deep, and
our brains are shallow.*
—RICHARD BAXTER

The practice of studying empowers us to unlock our calling
and fulfill our destiny. You don't wake up to a "eureka moment"
one day where everything about your calling, purpose, and
destiny magically makes sense and you are given a detailed
play-by-play of how you are supposed to fulfill these things over
the course of your life. In fact, I find it to be quite the opposite. We may have a sense of what we feel called to do or areas
we desire to influence, but there is a process of *unwrapping* our
calling through self-discovery and a lifestyle of study.

I know the word "study" doesn't sound appealing at first. I
invite you to step back and prepare to change your perspective. The "bad taste" that the word *study* produces is due to the
context we have placed it in since our earliest recollections of
school. Studying was not a gateway to personal success, prosperity, and abundance—at least, we did not see it that way.
Rather, it meant rigorous hours of reading and memorization
in order to secure us a favorable or, if not, at least a passing
grade on a test, quiz, or in a class. We must readjust how we
approach studying if we are going to walk in new levels of

intellectual abundance—as study is an essential key to unwrapping one's destiny.

It is impossible for you to grow and prosper apart from a rigorous commitment to learning. A casual approach to pursuing information will, in turn, produce casual corresponding results. Think of it this way. If we did minimal study for an exam in college, we would often receive a "minimal" grade. The level to which we go after knowledge determines the level to which that information will cause us to personally prosper. Now, I want to help you break out of the grade-driven paradigm you might still have concerning study.

In school, we studied to get grades. In life, we study to fulfill our purpose and maximize our potential. We study to progress. We study with clear vision that the information we are pursuing is not for the purpose of getting us a passing grade, but instead, empowering us to walk in new realms of success. Success is the fruit of study.

Of course, study by itself is not what causes us to succeed. One can be the most studied person (often labeled as "book smart") and still fail to put that learning into practice. However, study, when embraced with the mindset of a learner, is essential to ongoing growth and development. If we apply ourselves and dig deep into the topics we are studying, that knowledge will start to permeate deeply into the fabric of who we are. Study by itself does not change us; rather, it is our perspective of study that determines the benefits we receive from the practice.

Mozart said, "It is a mistake to think that the practice of my art has become easy to me. I assure you, dear friend, no one has given so much care to the study of composition as I. There is scarcely a famous master in music whose works I have not frequently and diligently studied." Genius, creativity, and expertise are living within us; however, they are released through study!

REFLECTION QUESTIONS

How have you thought about study in the past?

_____

_____

_____

_____

_____

_____

List some areas/items of interest that you would be willing to devote study to:

_____

_____

_____

_____

_____

_____

Why do you think study is necessary if you wish to succeed in any of these areas? (These questions are designed to help you change your perspective on studying; you need to make the clear connection between study and personal growth/success/prosperity.)

_____

_____

_____

_____

_____

_____

_____

ACTION STEPS

Until you know that life is interesting—and
find it so—you haven't found your soul.
—GEOFFREY FISHER

I hope that, by now, you have a slightly different perspective of studying. It is not your enemy, nor is it a necessary *evil*. Study is an essential common denominator to those who have gone on to experience tremendous success. The Bible implores you to, *"Study to shew thyself approved unto God, a workman that needeth not to be ashamed"* (2 Tim. 2:15 KJV).

Day Ten

WISDOM

Wisdom is the principal thing; therefore get wisdom.
And in all your getting, get understanding.
—PROVERBS 4:7

Wisdom is the supernatural ability to apply information at the right time, in the correct way, in order to prosper and succeed. We do not *learn* wisdom, per se. I have not heard of any classes that teach wisdom. The principles of good study and acquisition of information can certainly be taught; however, wisdom is developed through a much different process—it's called *the fear of the Lord.*

Scripture makes it clear that wisdom begins with the fear of the Lord (see Prov. 9:10). I talk about this at length in *The Prosperous Soul* book, so for the sake of time, I want to give you some practical teaching on the connection between wisdom and study (which you learned about yesterday).

Wisdom is what makes your study profitable. You cannot become wise without study, but neither will study make you wise. Study provides a knowledge base for wisdom to draw from. While study is the acquisition of information, wisdom is the application of study.

On the other hand, years of study will not necessarily translate into wisdom. There is a "wisdom from above" (see James 3:17) that is determined by our relationship with the Creator and Wise

King. He is wisdom personified and He has given us the *Spirit of wisdom* (see Isa. 11:2), who is the Holy Spirit living within us.

Take studying the Bible for example. There are many who have given their entire lives to gleaning theological information from the pages of Scripture, but they do not walk in wisdom. The Bible they study does not profit their everyday lives. To walk in wisdom is to *know* how to actually put what's written in the Bible to work in an everyday, relevant manner. One can approach the Bible as a textbook yet never benefit from the depth of revelation it offers.

God's Word is His divine blueprint to position you for prosperity in every realm of your life. It is not just about gaining health and wealth, as many have overly emphasized. Those are simply two aspects of the complete *Shalom* (Hebrew for *peace*) or *Sozo* (Greek for *salvation*) of God. Salvation is holistic in nature. It is multi-dimensional. There is no access into the Kingdom of God apart from your sins being forgiven and your spirit being born again through the work of Christ. This is fundamental; you cannot ever minimize it! The problem is that people are born again into a Kingdom that they know very little about.

What we are learning in *The Prosperous Soul* is how to live as successful Kingdom citizens. A key to walking in this supernatural citizenship is operating in the wisdom that God has made liberally and freely available to all who ask (see James 1:5).

Reflection Questions

Explain how you understand the difference between study and wisdom:

_____

_____

Read Proverbs 9:10. How is the *fear of the Lord* the beginning of wisdom? Write down your thoughts on this verse in the space below.

_____

_____

_____

_____

_____

_____

_____

_____

Why is your relationship with the Holy Spirit important to walking in wisdom?

_____

_____

_____

_____

_____

_____

ACTION STEPS

*If you need wisdom, ask our gener-
ous God, and he will give it to you.*
—JAMES 1:5 NLT

Wisdom can become a very abstract concept if we do not consistently keep it grounded and practical—yet this is how God meant
it to be taught—*practically.* Wisdom is your key to walking in good
success every single day of your life. No, it does not assure you a
trial-free, seamless coast through your remaining days on earth.
It *does* give you the ability to walk in victory, even when you are
experiencing opposition and difficulty. What is the key to accessing this supernatural wisdom? *Asking.*

Week Three

EMOTIONAL PROSPERITY

Guard your heart above all else,
for it determines the course of your life.
—PROVERBS 4:23 NLT

Day Eleven

JOY

Joy is the infallible sign of the presence of God.
—PIERRE TEILHARD DE CHARDIN

*I*t is typical for us to mistake happiness and joy. Happiness is often circumstance-dependent. In other words, we are happy just as long as our circumstances are favorable. Joy does not operate this way. Problematically, we assume that happiness and joy are one and the same. They are not. I believe that joy is the foundation to walking in emotional prosperity and wholeness.

Even though joy clearly has emotional expression, it is, above all, a fruit or characteristic of the Spirit-filled life in spite of circumstances. Many of us are familiar with the *Fruit of the Spirit* as defined by the apostle Paul in Galatians 5:22-23: *"But the fruit of the Spirit is love, joy, peace, longsuffering, kindness, goodness, faithfulness, gentleness, self-control."* These words remind us that what we are discussing is not a feeling; it is a fruit. It is not an emotional response or reaction; joy is the result of living a lifestyle yielded to the Holy Spirit.

Joy, however, is an emotional driver. If we discover how to live out of a place of joy, we can navigate through any season or situation because we are not living from our feelings. Instead, we are living from an ironclad, steadfast reality. The secret to living out of this reality is to *choose* joy.

Joy is a choice—as is peace. The enemy of your soul will try to steal your joy, but you can choose to resist him and remain in joy. There are few things more supernatural than witnessing a man or woman *living* from a place of deep, abiding joy. Talk to each one of them, and you will find their joy is not the result of living a life without conflict or trouble. Far from it. They have learned to pursue a far more valuable reality and walk in it. They recognize that the joy-*full* life far outweighs any fleeting pleasure, disappointment, or setback. Joy is constant. Joy is stable. Joy is deep contentment. To choose joy is to acknowledge God's presence in any given situation. Again, this perspective demands intentionality. By default, we tend to focus on problems rather than God's presence. To be joy-motivated, we must maintain a fixed gaze upon our ever-present and always faithful God.

This most exemplifies one who is living the prosperous soul lifestyle we are studying.

The Prosperous Soul book provides you with greater detail on what joy actually is. I want to help you experience it. Today, I want to help you get a running start on choosing a lifestyle of joy. Storms of hostility, bitterness, unwarranted criticism, negativity, strife, and the like may roar toward you, but if you choose joy and refuse to let go of it—picking a bigger paradigm view than one that only sees the temporary setbacks—you will be able to overcome them, or at least outlast them.

Fullness of joy is found in the presence of the Lord (see Ps. 16:11)—and it is His joy that gives us strength (see Neh. 8:10).

REFLECTION QUESTIONS

What is the difference between happiness and joy?

_____

_____

_____

Joy is a fruit of the Spirit, according to Galatians 5:22-23. What is the difference between a fruit of the Spirit and an emotional feeling/response?

_____

_____

_____

_____

_____

Do you currently live a joy-full life? Based on what you have read so far, what are some simple ways you can position yourself to walk in the *joy of the Lord* on a continuous, sustained basis?

_____

_____

_____

_____

_____

ACTION STEPS

For the joy of the Lord is your strength.
—NEHEMIAH 8:10

Go through the Scriptures, find key passages on joy, and make these your meditation. Remember, spiritual prosperity is not simply reading the Bible; that is the starting place. For you to truly understand the importance of joy in your life, I encourage you to locate three verses on joy and constantly think upon these truths. Place them wherever you will be reminded of their joy-releasing power. Your refrigerator. In your smartphone. Your computer screensaver. It is quality, not quantity, that transforms us.

Day Twelve

PEACE

The peace of God, which surpasses all understanding,
will guard your hearts and minds through Christ Jesus.
—PHILIPPIANS 4:7

The world that we currently live in is far from being peace-*full*. In fact, a sense of peace appears to be the one thing everyone wants, yet few possess—including believers just like you. Yet, every born-again child of God has the *Prince of Peace* living within them. You may not *feel* peaceful, but peace is not an emotion. Peace is another fruit of the Spirit. Nor is it a matter of trying to *get* peace. It's already yours in Christ. It is learning how to live from what you have already received in the Holy Spirit, as He has placed the very peace of God within you.

Paul tells us that a citizen of God's Kingdom is actually defined by righteousness, joy, and peace *in* the Holy Spirit. (See Romans 14:17.) This means that peace is actually found, experienced, and released *in* the person of the Holy Spirit. The Holy Spirit lives inside of you, so the very thing that nations so desperately need actually resides within *you*.

It is peace that causes you to stand firmly in your identity in Christ. It releases courage and stability when you are believing for answers that you have not yet seen come to pass. It keeps you grounded in the character, nature, and good plans of God. Peace is an anchor. It enables you to weather circumstances that would cause most to be shaken in their faith.

As you make the decision to walk in peace, drawing from the grace and strength of the Spirit of God within you, you will draw attention. People will take notice, both struggling believers and curious unbelievers. They will watch your walk and want to know what makes you different. You see, they have a predetermined paradigm for interacting with trouble, disappointment, problems, and struggles. Peace is only a concept to them, not a truth.

The Kingdom of God is marked by stability—a key hallmark of which is peace. If you are studying *anything* in a Kingdom context, you must remember that it is sure and solid, just like the King. Returning to Romans 14:17, the Kingdom of God is defined as *"righteousness, peace, and joy in the Holy Spirit."* If peace and joy are key cornerstone realities in the Kingdom, it goes without saying that they are stable. Everything in the world is shakable *except* the unshakable Kingdom of God (see Heb. 12:28) and its corresponding culture. Peace is a defining quality of Kingdom culture. Do you desire to *live* as a citizen of God's Kingdom? (You may *be* a citizen by identity, but are you living as one practically?) If you do, it means embracing and implementing a new perspective on peace.

So what is the key to walking in God's peace? You need to recalibrate how you apply the promises of God in your life. I want to help you do this today.

REFLECTION QUESTIONS

Can someone *be* a citizen of God's Kingdom but not actually *live* like a citizen? What does this look like?

How is peace in God's Kingdom different from the world's peace?

To what degree are *you* currently living a peace-full life?

ACTION STEPS

Peace I leave with you; my peace I give you. I
do not give to you as the world gives. Do not let
your hearts be troubled and do not be afraid.
—JOHN 14:27 NIV

I want to help you approach peace from a Kingdom perspective. In order to do this, you need to see God's promises in a new way. God's promises are keys to keeping your soul anchored in supernatural peace. Don't distance yourself from His promises, believing they are not available to you personally, or that you have to work hard for them, or that God is not interested in you. Those are lies. Jesus reminds us that He has *already* given you peace— *His* peace!

Have you believed any lies about God and His promises? If so, confront them now. Such deception could be preventing you from experiencing true peace in your life.

Day Thirteen

FORTITUDE

*Courage is the most important of all the
virtues because without courage, you can't
practice any other virtue consistently.*
—Maya Angelou

*B*ecause your soul represents the very core of your being, it is important you learn how to exercise control over the issues that flow out of your soul. This includes your emotions. Fortitude is the ability to exercise self-control and mastery over how you feel. It serves as an anchor in a world where emotions rule and feelings dominate—often leading to heartache, confusion, poor choices, and self-sabotage. So how do you exercise fortitude over your emotions?

First, it must be reinforced that God created you as an emotional being. It is wrong to believe that a cold, stoic disposition is more godly than feeling deeply. Consider this: God made you into a *feeling* person because He Himself has feelings—strong ones. Scripture is replete with examples of God Almighty exhibiting different emotional qualities. You see this with Jesus Christ, as He was moved with compassion for the sick and hurting.

Yet, one must ask, "If emotions are good, why do they cause so many problems?" Let's return to the Master as an example—the Lord Himself. God felt strongly about situations. He felt deeply grieved concerning your sin. His emotions responded time after time as His people, the Israelites, rebelled against Him throughout the Old Testament. God felt, yes, but He did not always respond to His feelings. Instead, God acts in agreement with His truth. Just read what the prophets wrote in the Old Testament. Here, we are given a glimpse into the emotional world of a God who is heartbroken over the sin of His people. The emotion is obviously pure. However, it is interesting to note that God does not respond irrationally to emotion. He feels, but those feelings do not lead Him to destroy Israel and start the work of creation over. They lead Him back to His Word. God does indeed punish Israel, but in such a manner that was in agreement with what had been prophesied concerning their fate (if they continued in rebellion). I reiterate, God responds to truth. The Spirit of God lives within you, enabling *you* to walk in the same measure of self-control over your emotional life (after all, self-control is a fruit of the Spirit).

I hope you see that the key to fortitude is not allowing your emotions to have free reign in your life, but rather for you to anchor your feelings through truth. This is what grants you fortitude when you are flooded with all sorts of emotions. Truth is the great discerner and evaluating agent of how you feel. Remember, not all emotions are trying to lead you astray. It is the Holy Spirit who enables you to recognize what you are feeling and help you discern whether or not a certain emotion is a feeling you should act on, or if you should cast it down and instead cling to the eternal standard of truth.

REFLECTION QUESTIONS

How do you understand God to be emotional? Can you think of any specific examples in Scripture where God/Jesus/Holy Spirit demonstrates emotion? Reflect on these stories and accounts, as they remind you that emotion is not your enemy!

Why do you think so many people (particularly Christians) think emotions are bad? How can emotions lead us astray in our decision-making ability?

What kind of power do your emotions have over your life? Do you find that they lead you into difficulty, or bring you into blessing/good decision-making?

ACTION STEPS

*Only be strong and very courageous, being
careful to do according to all the law that
Moses my servant commanded you.*
—JOSHUA 1:7 ESV

I want to remind you that *emotions are not bad.* They are from God. The problem is the external stimuli trying to manipulate your emotions. Remember, just because you feel strongly about something does not immediately give you license to act on that emotion. The feeling may be completely legitimate, but the context might be absolutely sinful and destructive. Consider lust. Within the context of marriage, the desire for one's spouse is God-designed and God-sanctioned. However, the same strong feelings outside of marriage are considered sinful. When the temptation comes, bringing with it different feelings and emotions, it is so important for you to be grounded in the truth so you know how to recognize what is of God, what is of your flesh, and what is of the evil one. As it was for Joshua, so it is for you—truth empowers you to be strong and courageous!

Day Fourteen

HOPE

*Now faith is the assurance of things hoped
for, the conviction of things not seen.*
—HEBREWS 11:1 ESV

ope is your blueprint for walking in God's blessing. It gives you a clear vision for where you are headed in life—and for what you've been authorized through Scripture to exercise your faith. In fact, without hope, it is impossible for you to walk in faith! This is true in every dimension of our lives.

For example, if you were never exposed to the hope of salvation found in the Gospel, you would not have been able to, by faith, give Jesus your heart and trust Him to be your Lord and Savior. Hope exposes you to a reality, while faith is what brings the reality to pass in your life. It personalizes it, making it a real *for you*. The problem is, people are trying to believe God for things that they have no hope for. They are merely parroting confessions, declarations, and prayers they have heard other people pray. Just because you say you are speaking or praying *in faith* does not mean that faith is being released. True faith is fueled by hope. Scripture makes this abundantly clear!

Faith is the *"assurance of things hoped for."* In the Christian world, we have spent a lot of time on the faith aspect of this verse, while neglecting the necessary and foundational hope dimension. Faith gives *substance* to the things *hoped for* (see Heb. 11:1 KJV). Substance is materiality. I know many of us are trying to exercise our faith to bring certain realities to pass in our lives. Sadly, we are often lacking the necessary foundation of hope. Hope exposes us to the unseen realm of what is available in God's Kingdom. Faith reaches into that realm and pulls out God's promises, releasing them into our lives.

Bible hope is not idle wishing. It is a joyful and confident expectation. When you are exposed to promises in Scripture, remember who the Promiser is. He has an eternally faithful reputation. We must consider every Bible reality from this perspective. What God reveals as available to you in His Word is not "dangling the carrot" to only pull it away, keeping you chasing an unattainable prize. This is not God's nature. He is good. He is loving. He is kind. He is compassionate. He desires for you to be thoroughly equipped for every good work (see 2 Tim. 3:17)—and His promises are supernatural resources to help you fulfill your divine purpose. For you to benefit from God's promises, you *must* attach hope to them. There must be a confident joyful expectation that God will deliver on what He promised to do. When we see promises from this vantage point, everything is positioned for us to exercise our faith.

Keep in mind that hope is specific. It does not simply assume everything will work out in the end. Hope has a very clear vision of a desired end. Yes, we trust God with the mechanics of *how* these results will ultimately come to pass. We do not direct or instruct God. At the same time, hope is not wishy-washy and vague. Even though the *how* of what we are believing God for may change, the *what* is steadfast. Peace. Healing. Joy. Family salvation. Provision. Deliverance. Freedom from bondage. These are just a few promises that Scripture makes available for you to hope for. It is completely legal for your hope to be specific just as long as there are specific promises in Scripture to reinforce your hope.

REFLECTION QUESTIONS

How do you now understand the difference between hope and faith? (Consider this in light of today's entry after reading the coinciding chapter in *The Prosperous Soul*.)

_____

_____

_____

_____

_____

What is the relationship between hope and God's promises, as revealed in the Bible?

_____

_____

_____

_____

_____

ACTION STEPS

For You are my hope; O Lord God, You are my trust
from my youth and the source of my confidence.
*—*PSALM 71:5 AMP

You can get hope-*full* today! Every promise of God introduces you to new possibilities. It is these very possibilities that awaken hope in your heart for a better tomorrow. Hope confronts whatever circumstances you are going through and reminds you, based on the authority of God's Word, there is a better way. The impossible *is* possible. There is an "other side" to your storm. God is with you and He will lead you through to victory. Again, I encourage you to find promises in Scripture that speak to whatever circumstance, situation, or impossibility you may be facing. Stand on His unshakable truth, as it will serve as an anchor for your emotions.

Day Fifteen

TENACITY

*Many of life's failures are people who did not realize
how close they were to success when they gave up.*
—THOMAS A. EDISON

*E*ach practice you have studied so far tends to build upon its predecessor. By default, hope produces a people of tenacity and it is tenacity that escorts you into receiving God's promises. Why, then, do there seem to be people who have hoped for a season, but instead of moving forward with tenacious faith, slipped back into hopelessness? The fire of tenacity was extinguished because of how they responded to adversity. This is where the rubber meets the road.

Thomas Edison rightly linked failure to those who gave up. Some of us mistakenly assume that to fail is to become a failure. This is not true. Others see opposition and adversity as some expression of failure. In other words, they had hope that God's promise would come to pass, and instead of experiencing immediate fulfillment, they were hit with more intense pressure. They consider this "failure" because instead of their desired end (promise fulfilled), they experienced the exact opposite—*hope deferred.*

Is it any wonder that Scripture reminds us that "*hope deferred makes the heart sick, but a desire fulfilled is a tree of life*" (Prov. 13:12 ESV)?

So the question is, *"How does tenacity actually sustain hope, preventing my heart from getting sick?"* Let me outline the process a little more, giving you some context for the relationship between hope and tenacity.

When you become more mindful of God's promises than your problems, hope actually infuses you. It gets into you and has trouble getting out. Hope apprehends you, producing a burning desire to see what you are hoping for come to pass. However, as you are discovering, it is possible for someone to start with hope, become discouraged, and never see the promise fulfilled. How can this be? They did not understand the tenacity required to *steward* their hope. Did you get that? We steward and ultimately sustain hope in our lives by exercising tenacity.

With hope being so powerful, how can people who have been exposed to God's promises end up falling short of receiving them? Show me a person who perseveres through adversity, and I will show you a person who receives the promises they've hoped for. The author of Hebrews writes, *"We do not want you to become lazy, but to imitate those who through faith and patience inherit what has been promised"* (Heb. 6:12 NIV).

Jesus reminds us to ask—and then keep on asking. He instructs us to knock and continue knocking. Some read these words and assume that God needs our reminding or is hard of hearing. Not at all. More than just using repetitious words in prayer or embracing a begging spirit, Jesus is encouraging us to persevere. This is your vital key to experiencing the rich life. Some assume that prosperity or richness means the absence of adversity. Not a chance. The prosperous soul is not problem-free; it is hope-full and tenacious. The prosperous soul presses through difficulty—perseveres—and receives the promises of God.

REFLECTION QUESTIONS

What is the relationship between hope and tenacity?

_____

_____

_____

_____

_____

_____

Describe the following statement: *Tenacity sustains hope.* How does having tenacity actually keep hope alive for you?

_____

_____

_____

_____

_____

_____

How have you personally responded to God's promises in your life? Are there any that you gave up on because of adversity? Journal your thoughts below.

_____

_____

_____

_____

_____

_____

ACTION STEPS

The Spirit of God, who raised Jesus
from the dead, lives in you.
—ROMANS 8:11 NLT

I want to see hope sustained in your life. This comes by exercising tenacity. Perhaps you have embraced a perspective that assumes *everything* that happens in your life is by God's divine design. This is a dangerous viewpoint, for it prevents us from persevering for God's promises. If we believe everything that happens is because of God's direct orchestration, we will not pray *against* what is happening for fear of challenging God's sovereign plan.

Good news. God is sovereign! However, there is also an enemy. Jesus came to give you abundant life, while the thief is out to steal, kill, and destroy. He especially delights in destroying hope. Today, I am praying that the Spirit of God will invade your life in a powerful way—and resurrect a hope you may have given up on because of adversity.

Week Four

PHYSICAL PROSPERITY

The greatest wealth is health.
—Virgil

Day Sixteen

THE SOUL-BODY CONNECTION

A merry heart does good, like medicine,
but a broken spirit dries the bones.
—PROVERBS 17:22

The body and the soul are directly linked. For us to neglect the body in favor of emphasizing the invisible dimensions, the soul and the spirit, is a travesty and must be avoided at all costs. We are spirit, soul, *and* body. Every part of our personhood is valuable to God, and thus demands focus and development. Though it is important for us to distinguish how each functions; the problem is that when we study the body, soul, or spirit individually, we tend to think that they operate disconnected from each other. They are one in the same way that the Lord our God is one—Father, Son, and Spirit. After all, we were created in the image of One who is three in one.

When you see each dimension of your personhood as separate, it is easy for you to believe that one does not directly impact the other. In other words, you think that the health of your soul does not impact the health of your body. This is a deadly deception. The more you are able to identify the link between soul and body, the more you will make the appropriate soul investments that produce returns in your physical health.

Dr. Don Colbert's book, *Deadly Emotions*, directly targets this integral relationship, providing a detailed analysis of how the state of your soul (mind, will, emotions) impacts the condition of your physical body. The impact of a single toxic emotion is startling. Yet many do not simply experience a single negative emotion; many live with unhealthy souls, which in turn produce unhealthy bodies. Of course, there are physical factors that impact your health as well—diet, exercise, lifestyle, genetics, etc. That is an entirely different subject of discussion. Today, we'll explore the impact of your soul on your body's physiology.

Even though an unhealthy soul can do great damage to your physical health, the opposite is also true. The prosperous soul, by default, can produce a healthy physical body. The specifics concerning this, as well as some brief excerpts from the medical community, are presented in *The Prosperous Soul* book.

The goal for today is to help you understand the body-soul connection and the importance of investing in the health of your soul. Many Christians tend to focus exclusively on the spirit realm. We read our Bibles. We attend church services. We pray. We invest in our spiritual well-being because we desire our spiritual walk with the Lord to be robust and healthy. This is fundamental, but here is the problem: We do not see every realm of our person as interconnected.

Did you know that your spiritual life is supposed to impact your soul, and that your soul is designed to impact your body? We cannot live segmented lives. Jesus died to give you a very holistic salvation. As you seed the Word of God into your spirit, you should also expect it to powerfully impact your soul. You will think differently. You will deal with emotions differently. Your attitude will change.

Your soul life is influenced by the investments you are making in your spiritual life. As your soul life is enriched, you should likewise expect your soul to produce an equally powerful impact on your physical health.

REFLECTION QUESTIONS

Describe your understanding of humankind being a three-part person—body, soul, and spirit.

_____

_____

_____

_____

_____

_____

What impact does your soul have on your physical health? How have you experienced this impact in your own life?

_____

_____

_____

_____

_____

_____

Why do you think it is important to have a prosperous soul if you want to be enriched physically?

_____

_____

_____

_____

_____

_____

ACTION STEPS

A sad soul can kill you quicker, far quicker, than a germ.
—JOHN STEINBECK

Today, I want you to take a brief "soul cleanse" (for more about this, see my book *The 40 Day Soul Fast*). Try to identify anything in your soul that might be negative or harmful and thus be contributing to a poor state of physical health. Write one of these down and target it in the days ahead. The key to experiencing progress is taking one step at a time. Don't try to find every single problem that is wrong with you. Often, God shields us from being aware of certain things as He does not want to overwhelm us. He takes us through life, one step at a time, targeting one growth area at a time.

Day Seventeen

SELF-CONTROL

*A person without self-control is like a
city with broken-down walls.*
—PROVERBS 25:28 NLT

What is the dangerous thing about a city with broken-down walls? It is positioned for enemy conquest. Without self-control, we become easy prey for the destructive schemes of our adversary.

More than anything, the absence of self-control reveals a lack of vision. Consider Proverbs 19:18, which states, *"Where there is no vision, the people perish"* (KJV). Another translation says that where there is no vision, the people are unrestrained. Those who live without restraint will ultimately perish in every dimension of life. If we do not exercise self-control in an area of our lives, by default that specific area will suffer. It becomes a broken-down wall that is vulnerable to invasion, conquest, and potential destruction.

The key to self-control is *vision*. This is especially true when it comes to living in physical prosperity. No other area of our lives requires as much self-control as does the care of our physical bodies. In the next few days, we will be addressing some of those topics that no one likes to talk about—diet and exercise. The very mention of these words fills some of us with anxiety and dread. Why? Because we *know* we need to do them, and oftentimes they come with the discomfort of restrictions, sore muscles, and a lot of inconvenience.

To get beyond the resistance you may feel in the present moment, you need a vision. Rather than focusing on the journey, focus on the destination. Rather than focusing on what you can't have now, focus on what you will have later. You need a vision for the systems you'll put in place, the routines and habits you'll develop, the goals you'll achieve, and the rewards you'll reap. That vision is what keeps you self-controlled. Conversely, living without vision—and therefore without self-control—keeps you trapped in a perpetual cycle of failure and frustration.

I believe God wants to show you how to live better so you'll live longer. But He will not *force* you to exercise self-control, or any other fruit of the Spirit for that matter. However, self-control, as with every other fruit of the Spirit, will enable you to live a richer life. The key is having a vision for what you want to accomplish, and then creating an action plan to complete that vision.

Divide your desired outcomes into immediate and long-range rewards and practice choosing the latter. You'll need to put work before pleasure, exercise before relaxing, reading before television, prayer before gossip, virtue before vice, and the like, every time. Use self-control to practice wholeness. Don't overwork, sacrificing family time and health to inch ahead in your career. Use self-control to manage your health for strength, energy, and long life; your money to be enough to care for all of your real needs (we'll talk more about that in the last section of this book); your time and skills to increase the value of each minute you work; and how you rest and recreate to get the most out of your family time or to recharge your batteries.

REFLECTION QUESTIONS

How do you think self-control has a direct impact on your physical body?

What are some key signs of a life *without* self-control?

Can you think of some specific areas in your life where you'd like to practice more self-control? List them below.

ACTION STEPS

*Those who are at the mercy of impulse—who lack
self-control—suffer moral deficiency: The ability to
control impulse is the base of will and character.*
—DANIEL GOLEMAN
Emotional Intelligence

Identify areas in your life where you feel you should exercise more self-control. Now, instead of feeling bad about poor decisions you've made, be proactive. Ask yourself, *"What is my vision?"* Most likely, the areas where you have been without self-control are suffering. This is not God's best for your life! His plan is *abundant* life. However, you must position yourself for abundance. This starts with having a vision. How do you want these areas of your life to look? The best template to serve as a blueprint is God's Word.

Day Eighteen

EXERCISE AND NUTRITION

Good for the body is the work of the body, and
good for the soul is the work of the soul, and
good for either is the work of the other.
—HENRY DAVID THOREAU

*I*f you do not recognize the benefits of self-control, exercise and nutritious eating will be impossible. Yes, I believe all things are possible with God. At the same time, you are a co-laborer with God. He will not "do it" for you. He gives you grace, strength, and anointing. He gives you wisdom to make good decisions. And yes, He also gives you the Holy Spirit to empower you to walk in self-control. This is *very* important. You don't need to pray for self-control as much as you need to thank God for already giving it to you through the Holy Spirit (because it is a fruit of the Spirit as listed in Galatians 5).

The necessity of exercise and nutrition is clearly laid out in *The Prosperous Soul* book. These are vehicles that help take you back to God's original intent for healthy, abundant living. Humankind has come a long way since the Garden of Eden. The advances have been phenomenal, but also the setbacks are equally as stunning. When I say "setbacks," I am specifically referring to the lifestyle many have embraced regarding how to eat and manage their lives.

People have never been as sedentary as they are today. In theory, one would never have to leave their bed to complete a full day of "work." The occasional trip to the kitchen is all that is required. Add to this sedentary way of being what we find in our kitchens! Worse still is when the trip to the kitchen is replaced by a quick journey to the drive-thru window.

Don't feel condemned about this. Condemnation never leads to transformation. Remember, self-control begins with vision, and without a vision you will continue perishing, little by little, through unrestrained bad habits.

So I encourage you, go back to the first two chapters of Genesis and rediscover how humankind lived before sin entered the picture. I realize we can't go back to the Garden of Eden, but it's worthwhile to consider the context. Adam and Eve spent all of their time being active; they were not sedentary in the least. There were no television sets, armchairs, or couches. They also ate off the land. This was not a restriction, but rather a blessing. God had made an abundance of living food for them to eat. It grew directly out of God's rich soil and was filled with all of the nutrients that He intended.

Exercise and healthy eating habits actually help us return to God's original blueprint for humanity—at least, to the best of our ability in the twenty-first century. His purpose is for us to be strong and healthy. God does not desire for His people to be weak and sick. The picture we're given of Eden is a powerful illustration of who God is and what He desires for His children. It is a glimpse of His best and of our ideal lifestyle.

So, *what is the key to experiencing victory in your diet and fitness? Vision.* How would you like to feel in the future? How would you like to look in the future? What size are you? Are you sick and tired—or are you fit, healthy, and filled with energy? The strength and clarity of your vision will determine your measure of commitment.

Yesterday, you identified some physical areas where you needed to exercise self-control. That only comes through having a clear vision of the change you want to produce. Now, I want to help you come up with a strategy for healthy eating and exercise. I am going to make this very simple. My goal is to help you start the process and stick with it, even when you feel like giving up.

REFLECTION QUESTIONS

Why do you think so many people are frustrated when it comes to diet and fitness?

_____

_____

_____

_____

_____

Why do you think fitness and healthy eating are important to fulfilling God's plan and purpose for your life?

_____

_____

_____

_____

_____

How does having a clear vision help you remain committed to eating right and exercising regularly?

_____

_____

_____

_____

Action Steps

Where there is no vision, the people are unrestrained.
—Proverbs 29:18 nasb

Once again, the key here is to take one step at a time. Every small step advances you toward your vision. Don't overwhelm yourself with obligations. Start *somewhere* and celebrate your progress. Increase your goals only as you are able. And remember, you are what you eat!

Write down what you would like to see happen in your life in the areas of eating and fitness. Take this time to brainstorm. Talk/listen to God. Consider how you would like to experience transformation.

Day Nineteen

REST

*And on the seventh day God ended His work
which He had done, and He rested on the seventh
day from all His work which He had done.*
—Genesis 2:2

Rest is an alien concept to many of us.

You can sleep but not experience true rest. Unfortunately, many people are not getting the quality or quantity of sleep that will usher them into truly restorative rest.

Here is a good evaluator that will help determine what kind of rest you are getting. Ask yourself, *"How do I feel at the end of the day?"* Are you dragging yourself home to eat, spending a little time with your family before zoning out in front of the TV, then falling into bed to get up the next morning and start the cycle all over again? Do you go to bed tired and awaken just as tired?

If this describes your relationship with "rest," it is time for you to step into God's *better* plan. *The Prosperous Soul* book explains what rest is, God's design for rest, and why it is important. Now, I want to help you personally experience what you read about.

First, rest enables you to function in the image and likeness of the Creator. He rested and expects you to do likewise. Further still, He has empowered you with His very Spirit to imitate Him. The apostle Paul encourages us to be *"imitators of God"* (Eph. 5:1 ESV). If this is so, then we are to imitate the God who *rested*.

Second, you are able to rest because the Spirit of God lives within you. He produces the character and nature of God in your life. You cannot simply imitate God through willpower—this is a supernatural process. The marvelous truth is that this supernatural power is already yours. Draw from the endless well of the Holy Spirit within you and learn how to live every moment in divine rest.

Third, rest is the result of peace. Peace is a fruit of the Spirit. You don't need to beg God for peace; it is yours in the Holy Spirit. We reviewed this earlier, but it bears repeating. Peace is an essential element in God's Kingdom. Remember, the Kingdom is defined by righteousness, peace, and joy. (See Romans 14:17.) *Peace* is what causes you to enter into rest.

One of the most important truths for you to meditate on that releases the rest of God in your life is simply this: *You are in right standing with God.*

Rest comes from your security in Christ. Yes, there are a million things you *could* be doing every day. Have a plan. Do what needs to be done. Accomplishment is important. However, if at the end of the day you cannot enter into a state of rest, your perspective *throughout the day* was off. God doesn't want you to only rest at night. Rest should permeate your lifestyle. As you are working, you can be in a state of rest. As you are going about your business, you can be resting. How? By being present with the Holy Spirit—living every moment in God's presence. We know that God is with us. He is working on our behalf. He is moving behind the scenes. His will is coming to pass. You live in a constant state of trusting your faithful and loving heavenly Father. *This* is what positions us to live in rest.

Focus on who God is, what He has done for you through Christ, and how He is working in your life every moment of every day.

REFLECTION QUESTIONS

How is it possible to sleep without being at rest? Have you ever personally experienced this? Describe your experience below.

_____

_____

_____

_____

_____

_____

Why is the Holy Spirit so important in helping you learn how to rest? What role do you think He plays in your state of rest? (Based on what you have read.)

_____

_____

_____

_____

_____

In what ways can you experience rest by meditating on what Jesus has done for you?

_____

_____

_____

_____

ACTION STEPS

*So there is a special rest still waiting for the people of
God. For all who have entered into God's rest have
rested from their labors, just as God did after creating the world. So let us do our best to enter that rest.*
—HEBREWS 4:9-11 NLT

Today, I encourage you to meditate on what Jesus has done for
you. This truth alone has the power to continually usher you into
supernatural rest. Don't let this be a one-time experience. There
are some amazing promises in the Bible that specifically address
the topic of rest. I encourage you to look them up. However, the
most powerful truths that release rest are those that point to the
rest found in Christ.

The author of Hebrews wrote that the Old Testament looked
forward toward a future time of rest for the people of God.
Because of what Jesus accomplished on the cross for you, this rest
is available now—as well as for all eternity.

PURITY

*If the spiritual bloom of our life with God is getting
impaired in the tiniest degree, we must leave off
everything and get it put right. Remember that vision
depends on character—the pure in heart see God.*
—OSWALD CHAMBERS
Referring to MATTHEW 5:8

*P*urity is a word directly associated with morality; thus
protecting society in general and individuals in particular on multiple dimensions.

Because we are focusing on physical prosperity this week, I
want to show you how purity actually leads you into dimensions
of abundance. That's right. Purity is not just about personal discipline, restraints and restrictions; it is about protection from
heartache, pain, disease, emotional destruction, and yes, even the
possibility of death.

John reminds us that the commandments of God are not bur-
densome. (See 1 John 5:3 NIV.) They should never be used as tools
for legalistic restriction. Anyone who seeks to please God should
want to come with *"clean hands and a pure heart...."* (Psalm 24:4).
Again, I come back to the importance of having a vision, and the
commitment to say "no" to the wrong so that you can say "yes"
to the right. If we are told, "Be pure...pursue purity," but are not
given a clear vision of what kind of blessing a lifestyle of purity

can release, we will be less inclined to live that way. A generation has been told to "be pure," but they have not been given a clear picture of *why* purity is so important.

Purity is more than sexual abstinence until marriage (although this is a key way to experience purity). Above all, purity is saying "yes" to God and "no" to the world's system. It is following God even when it seems like an entire culture is going in the opposite direction. It is in decisions such as these where we must be fueled by vision. Do not misunderstand me; God deserves our unqualified devotion, vision or no vision. He will often call you to do things you cannot wrap your mind around, but your heart will be at rest and peace.

Yet, God, being who He is, has not left us alone. He lives inside of us. Jesus told us that part of the relationship we get to enjoy with God is a friend-to-friend exchange of communication. God gives us instructions, but He also gives us a vision or reason for the instruction. Jesus explains, *"No longer do I call you servants, for a servant does not know what his master is doing; but I have called you friends, for all things that I heard from My Father I have made known to you"* (John 15:15). The Message Bible phrases the last part this way: *"I've let you in on everything I've heard from the Father."*

God gives you vision as to why purity is not only the acceptable path for you to follow, but why it is the *only* path that leads to true life, wholeness, peace, success, and prosperity. To go the way of the world is spiritual suicide. (See Colossians 2:20-23.) To choose any option other than God's option is to position yourself for failure—be it immediate or pending. God, being all-knowing, calls you into a life of purity as a way to guide you along His perfect path.

- Purity positions you to experience God's promises.

- Purity protects you from the enemy's snares.

- Purity guards your heart from becoming wrapped up in a dangerous soul tie.

- Purity keeps you from going places that could be harmful or destructive.

- Purity chooses company that builds you up, encourages you, and sharpens you, instead of leading you into sin and making poor choices.

- Purity upholds truth and rejects compromise.

- Purity rejects substandard living in favor of pursuing the abundant life that Jesus made available.

I pray that by now you see that purity is not a hardship; it actually protects you from evil and helps you live the prosperous life you were designed for. Make a promise to God, and to yourself, that you will live a life of purity. Renew your promise daily. Decide where you're going to draw the line, and tell God that with his help, you are not going to cross that line. If you are married, promise God that you will live true to your marriage vows. If you are single, promise God that you will live a life of purity until you are married. It is a serious thing to make a vow to God. Your integrity depends on keeping your end of the bargain. Here is the encouraging thing—God will empower you to do so day by day.

Remember, at the end of the day, whether you immediately experience a direct benefit of pursuing purity or not, obedience to God is worth it all.

REFLECTION QUESTIONS

How have you thought about the topic of purity in the past?

_____

_____

_____

List some different areas (besides sexuality) where you can walk in purity.

In what ways does purity protect you?

ACTION STEPS

Blessed are the pure in heart, for they shall see God.
—MATTHEW 5:8

Change the way you think about purity today. One thing I noted earlier is that purity positions you to walk in and experience

God's promises. This is absolutely true and vital for you to not only pursue purity, but enjoy the pursuit. Ask the Holy Spirit to help you see purity as a precious treasure. I encourage you to go ahead and write down every way that purity *serves you*. We know it honors God. That tends to be the common response. I want you to consider how a lifestyle of purity actually positions you to experience physical prosperity!

Week Five

RELATIONAL PROSPERITY

*The meeting of two personalities is like the
contact of two chemical substances: If there
is any reaction, both are transformed.*
—C.G. Jung

Day Twenty-One

EMPATHY

But when He (Jesus) saw the multitudes, He was moved with compassion for them, because they were weary and scattered, like sheep having no shepherd.
—MATTHEW 9:36

We cannot confuse sympathy and empathy. It is amazing how our good intentions (through sympathy and compassion) can actually keep people trapped in their cycles of bondage and struggle instead of empowering them to take responsibility for their own lives. This is not meant to sound harsh. Sympathy encourages people, yes. But it tends to encourage them *in* their struggles instead of building them up until they are able to not only experience victory, but also to *sustain* victory. This is the empowering force of empathy.

In Stephen Covey's highly acclaimed book, *The 7 Habits of Highly Effective People*, he encourages us to seek to understand rather than to be understood. This is the art of seeing from someone else's vantage point, or better stated, "walking a mile in someone else's shoes." Harper Lee, in her book *To Kill A Mockingbird* said it this way, "You never really understand a person until you consider things from his point of view.... Until you climb inside of his skin and walk around in it."

Empathy sees life through someone else's lenses, and without prejudice or bias seeks to understand. It also recognizes both the need and the individual's ability to respond to their need. For a deeper understanding, let's contrast sympathy with empathy. When sympathy acts, it tends to create emotional dependency. Sympathy "does *for* us," while leaving us powerless to do for ourselves. Empathy, on the other hand, comes alongside us and with compassion empowers us to experience victory for ourselves—and then actually sustain what we received. It is the proverbial "teaching a man to fish" rather than just giving him fish. Empathy props you back up on your two feet, and shows you how to start walking for yourself. Sympathy hands you crutches and says, "I'm so sorry this has happened to you." Empathy says, "I can only imagine how it must have felt, but you don't need to be in this state anymore. Let's get you walking out your dreams and vision—here are the tools." I want to help you recognize the difference between sympathy and empathy so that you can be a source of empowerment in your relationships. This is truly following the example of Jesus.

Jesus was often moved by compassion. However, this compassion was not idle. Compassion moved Him to step into people's lives and provide empowering solutions for their troubles. Consider the miracles of Jesus. Even though He stepped in and performed the supernatural on behalf of those in great need, He often invited the hurting person into his or her miracle. He involved people in their breakthroughs. Why?

Perhaps Jesus was giving us a prophetic picture of what the *life to come* would look like. The *life to come* is not Heaven in this context; it is the Christian life that we are all empowered to walk in because of the resurrected Christ.

A day was coming when Jesus would ascend to Heaven, but, as promised, He would not leave His people as orphans. Even though many of us assume that having Jesus *here*—live and in Technicolor—would be an unparalleled experience, Jesus actually said that it would be to our *advantage* that He left so He could send the Comforter, the Holy Spirit. (See John 16:7.) Surely this perplexed the disciples. Jesus, on the other hand, was giving them a blueprint for a richer life.

In Matthew 9:36, we see that Jesus was *"moved with compassion"* for the people *"because they were weary and scattered, like sheep having no shepherd."* One of the reasons that Jesus was moved with compassion for the people was that they were powerless (*weary*). They were weary of being taught, but not empowered. They were burdened by laws, rules, and regulations, but had no solutions. Jesus felt strongly toward these people, but was intent on not leaving them the same way they came. He healed and delivered the people, yes, but then, as you see with the twelve disciples, and later with the seventy He sent out—and ultimately, with every believer, starting with the Great Commission—Jesus had always been set on bringing the powerless into a place of being power-full.

REFLECTION QUESTIONS

How do you understand the difference between sympathy and empathy?

_____

_____

_____

_____

_____

What is the danger of only having sympathy?

_____

_____

_____

_____

In what ways do you exhibit empathy in your life? (In your relationships?) Do you feel that you extend more empathy or sympathy?

ACTION STEPS

Compassion hurts. When you feel connected to every-
thing, you also feel responsible for everything. And
you cannot turn away. Your destiny is bound with
the destinies of others. You must either learn to carry
the universe or be crushed by it. You must grow
strong enough to love the world, yet empty enough to
sit down at the same table with its worst horrors.
—ANDREW BOYD

Identify key relationships where you might need to make the shift from sympathy to empathy. Write down the names of these individuals, pray for them, pray for your ability to interact with them appropriately, and start putting true compassion into practice. You will be amazed to discover the measure of grace that comes to empower you when you simply step out to follow Jesus's example.

Day Twenty-Two

FORGIVENESS

Anyone can…tell a wounded person to "get over it," but that is not the answer that Christ brings. He reaches into the deepest places of our hearts and does a deep work of healing that allows us to forgive and even pray that those who wronged us will not have to experience God's fierce wrath.
—SHELLEY HUNDLEY[1]

Forgiveness is not flippant, nor is it feeling-based. We don't forgive only when we *feel* like forgiving, nor can we assume that the process is as easy as some make it out to be. "Just get over it." "Forgive, even when it doesn't make sense." "Just make the decision to forgive!"

These messages are not wrong, in and of themselves. Yes, we forgive when we don't feel like forgiving. Of course, we need to get over the hurt and pain that an offender has caused us, lest we end up living in bitterness. However, we need to reexamine the *process* of forgiveness in order to experience true spiritual growth, freedom, and wholeness in our relationships.

First, forgiveness is not merely making a concentrated effort to "forget" the bad that was done to you; it recognizes certain feelings are legitimate. It is not what happens to you that is the consideration here. It is what you do with what happens to you. As one created in God's image and likeness, you do actually experience the legitimate feelings of your Maker when you are wronged—justice and the need for retribution. Don't just assume that because you feel this way, you are falling into sin. It is responding to these feelings in an appropriate way that sets you up to freely release forgiveness.

Second, forgiveness is more than a decision—it is a legal procedure in the Kingdom of Heaven. There is only One Righteous Judge who sees and knows all. And this is the context in which *true* forgiveness is understood. Forgiveness recognizes that recompense must be made, but does so in a way that releases the offending person from being the one who suffers for it.

Third, keep in mind that there was One who *already* suffered for every offense *ever* committed. Recompense was made. The Judge rendered full judgment upon Christ, who willingly embraced the full wrath and payment of every single trespass ever committed. Thus, provision was made for all to be forgiven and become reconciled to the Judge, who is also the Father. Not all receive this provision, unfortunately.

Finally, the cross helps you maintain the right perspective on sin, forgiveness, and justice. Consider what the cross purchased for *you*. You are able to freely give only what you have freely received. Jesus gave the blueprint for forgiveness in *The Lord's Prayer* when He told us to pray in this manner: *"Forgive us our sins, as we have forgiven those who sin against us"* (Matt. 6:12 NLT). Our willingness to forgive reveals the depth of our understanding concerning God's forgiveness toward us.

If you struggle with forgiving anyone for anything, I encourage you to take a meditative trip back to the cross and consider the extreme manner in which the Judge forgave you. Holding unforgiveness, resentment, hatred, and bitterness in your heart for and toward anyone, particularly those that have abused, hurt, or offended you, is like drinking poison and hoping they would die. Forgiveness is not for them—it is for you. Why would you give someone or something permission to live in your mind without paying rent?

Scripture says that you were once an enemy of God because of your sin and offenses. (See Romans 5:8-10.) And yet, while you were living in open rebellion against Him, Christ died for you and God forgave you of *all* your sins. This is the ultimate pattern for forgiveness. Forgiveness is not about forgetting what has happened, it is about severing the emotional and psychological ties by releasing them to the Lord. As long as negative feelings remain and the thought of that individual flashes in your mind, you have not forgiven. Forgiveness is a process. Every time this happens, call their name and say, "I release you from my mind and spirit." It may take months or even years (see Matthew 18:22), but one day you will awaken with freedom. I know because I had to do this myself. The measure to which we live mindful of the forgiveness we have received is directly proportional to the measure of forgiveness we offer others in our everyday lives.

REFLECTION QUESTIONS

How is Christ dying on the cross a picture of God's perfect justice being served for every wrong and offense ever committed?

_____

_____

_____

_____

_____

What does *considering the cross* look like to you?

_____

_____

_____

_____

_____

_____

What is your understanding of forgiveness as a legal procedure in the Kingdom of Heaven? In what ways has retribution
already been served for the offenses committed against you? In
what ways can you trust God for future justice while releasing the
offender through forgiveness? Who do you have to forgive? Please
be specific.

_____

_____

_____

_____

_____

ACTION STEPS

But if we confess our sins to him, he is faithful and just to
forgive us our sins and to cleanse us from all wickedness.
—1 JOHN 1:9 NLT

Justice is satisfied through Jesus's sacrifice on the cross. It is
justice that allows Him to forgive us. It is also justice that allows
us to receive those we would accuse and look to God for recompense instead.

This is a process, though. We must continue to give our hurts
to God. Just because we commit to forgive someone once, twice,
or even several times, this does not promise that feelings of unforgiveness will not come back to bother us. The key is reminding
those emotions and feelings of the truth. We declare, "I gave that

to God and I don't have it anymore. I have forgiven that person." We stand upon the truth of the decision we made. To forgive is not a feeling. If we waited to forgive someone when we felt like it, we would never forgive.

1. Shelly Hundley, *A Cry for Justice* (Lake Mary, FL: Charisma House, 2011), 150, 155.

KINDNESS

*Don't you see how wonderfully kind, tolerant,
and patient God is with you? Does this mean
nothing to you? Can't you see that his kindness
is intended to turn you from your sin?*
—ROMANS 2:4 NLT

Kindness is a decision. Reflect on the account you read about in *The Prosperous Soul* book today. You saw a powerful glimpse of how King David extended kindness toward the crippled Mephibosheth.

Naturally speaking, David *could* have allowed bitterness and offense to drive him to take retribution upon this man for everything he suffered because of his grandfather, Saul. You'd better believe that Mephibosheth expected such judgment from David. There is even good evidence to support that Mephibosheth actually grew up fearing David, perhaps even despising him for taking the throne that should have come down to him. From this text I learned that kindness is as kindness does.

But David responded differently. He showed kindness to Mephibosheth. David's response most likely caught him off guard: *"Do not fear, for I will surely show you kindness for Jonathan your father's sake, and will restore to you all the land of Saul your grandfather; and you shall eat bread at my table continually"* (2 Sam. 9:7). Reflect on David's language for a moment: *I will surely show you kindness.* Kindness is not a feeling; it is a demonstration of will. It is a choice.

I will show kindness. By extending kindness, you are not responding to what someone deserves; rather, you are operating out of the nature of the One living within you. This is how God behaves, and He expects you to follow suit. Remember, *kindness* is one of the fruits of the Holy Spirit. (See Galatians 5:22-23.) You can draw from this characteristic of the Holy Spirit because His empowering presence lives within you. He makes it possible for you to say, like David, "*I will show kindness.*"

Kindness is a fruit of the Spirit because it is supernatural in nature. You are demonstrating the very character of God when you demonstrate kindness when kindness is not deserved. Consider this—it was God's kindness that brought you to repentance. This provides a powerful illustration of how and when kindness is extended.

God gave you kindness when you did not deserve it. In fact, He was kind to you *before* you ever came into the Kingdom. Kindness was God's divine tool of bringing you to a place of godly sorrow over your sin. Note, it is kindness, not condemnation. Kindness brings you to repentance because you are overwhelmed at His goodness—and in light of His goodness and perfection, you catch a glimpse of your sinful condition. You want nothing more to do with such a lesser way of living because of the overwhelming kindness God extended—the sacrifice He ultimately made on the cross. The Holy Spirit woos you to Christ using kindness.

What does this speak to us? We are to demonstrate kindness to those who are less than deserving. We certainly were. This is a powerful witness to the nature of God and reveals that we are partaking in His divine nature. (See 2 Peter 1:4.)

The world understands kindness as an "I'll scratch your back if you scratch mine." Kindness is returned for kindness. On the other hand, if someone is unkind, then the response from the other person tends to be either equally or more unkind. One feeling triggers an equal if not worse expression. This is not the way of the Spirit; this is the way of the flesh.

You don't need to live this way. You have the power within you, in the Holy Spirit, to return unkindness for kindness. If someone mistreats you, cuts you off in traffic, gossips behind your back, takes your parking place—whatever it may be—you have the power within you to make a supernatural decision: *I will choose to be kind!*

REFLECTION QUESTIONS

What makes David's act of kindness toward Mephibosheth so unusual? How is this a picture of how you are to extend kindness toward each other?

How do people in the world understand kindness versus someone who is living in God's Kingdom?

Meditate on Romans 2:4. What does God's expression of *kindness* show you about what kindness should look like in your life?

_____

_____

_____

_____

_____

_____

ACTION STEPS

Let all bitterness, wrath, anger, clamor, and evil
speaking be put away from you, with all malice.
And be kind to one another, tenderhearted, forgiv-
ing one another, even as God in Christ forgave you.
—EPHESIANS 4:31-32

You can be kind to people even when the situation, by all natural means, deserves unkindness. Just remember the Father's kindness toward you. While you did not deserve His kindness, He was kind to you. In fact, His kindness was so lavish and relentless that it was the very thing that brought you into repentance and new life in Christ. Maybe God wants to accomplish the same thing through you? Never underestimate the supernatural power of kindness. You are, after all, God's ambassador, sent into the world to reconcile the lost to the Father! Maybe, just maybe, your simple act of kindness will reveal the God who, *through kindness,* will introduce that person to who He really is. Here is a declaration you can make daily: I choose kindness. I will be kind to the poor, orphans, and widows, for they are alone. I will give to those who can never repay the favor. I choose to be kind to those who others perceive as mean, for they are afraid. I will be kind to those who mistreat others— the unkind and un-lovable, for such is how God treated me.

Day Twenty-four

GOODNESS

*Do your little bit of good where you are; it's those little
bits of good put together that overwhelm the world.*
—DESMOND TUTU

*I*f kindness is the action, goodness is the foundation that provides the motive to act with kindness. Unfortunately, our world is ripe with hindrances that short-circuit the flow of goodness. Perhaps we would see an increased frequency of acts of kindness, in both the Church and in society as a whole, if the following barriers were broken down.

Let's consider some of the barriers and identify strategies to demolishing them:

Barrier #1: Cynicism

When we are cynical of each another, it is nearly impossible for us to choose to extend good will. You need to be intentional about looking for the good, not the bad. Society at large does not encourage us to look for the good. It seems we are naturally wired to amplify the negative. News networks focus on every negative expression of humanity possible—murder, theft, greed, manipulation, sexual deviancy, etc. We are bombarded with constant reminders of why we should *not* trust people. The answer is to see like God does. Remember, even in our sin and rebellion, God chose us, He loved us, and He demonstrated His lavish kindness toward us.

Barrier #2: Bad Experiences

What gives birth to cynicism in your life? Bad experiences. As a result, you'll have a tendency to become leery of the trustworthiness of people. You'll question their motives. You'll be skeptical because you've been let down in the past. You gave money to the homeless person who ended up using your hard-earned dollars to buy drugs. You believed in a leader who let you down. A friend abandoned you, a family member abused you, a coworker betrayed you. The lens through which you see people is formed by your past experiences. Resist broad-brushing humanity based on the flaws of the few. We *all* have flaws. Yet we also *all* possess the capacity to do great things! Let's focus on one another's great capacities rather than each other's flaws.

Barrier #3: Identity

When we measure people by their sin, we will respond to them accordingly. And we are hindered in helping people *expect* to express the goodness of God in their own lives. When we measure people by their capacity to demonstrate goodness instead of how sinful they are, our response strategy changes. In order to call people into new levels of goodness, the worst thing for us to do is focus on the bad, the sin, and the negative. This is not a call to blind ourselves to the harmful and, yes, disastrous effect of sin. At the same time, when we constantly speak to people or talk about people like they *are no-good sinners*, we are feeding that identity more. We must call them into the goodness they were created to reveal and release.

For those who don't know Christ yet, their nature is to sin. That makes sense. Even so, we need to see these people and respond to them as men and women created in the image of God—a good God, at that. As we do this, our witness to the world changes. Instead of bringing condemnation, we are calling them up higher into the richer life and showing them a more accurate view of who God is.

For you as a believer, your nature has been changed. You are a new creation. For you to treat your brothers and sisters in the Lord like they are sinners by nature is to speak to the unrenewed, carnal parts of their lives and draw attention away from their status in Christ. Approach them as saints, not sinners. This is far more effective than berating them for *not* modeling the goodness of God. Instead of speaking to their shortcomings, call out their potential for Christlikeness. We are iron sharpening iron, and vice versa. While we need to call things out, it is absolutely essential that we create a culture of calling each other *up*.

This will produce a people who truly carry and exemplify the goodness of God in the earth.

REFLECTION QUESTIONS

How do goodness and kindness work together?

_____

_____

_____

_____

_____

Why is it important for you to be more focused on goodness than the sin in people's lives (especially those who are Christians)?

_____

_____

_____

_____

What happens when we focus more on a person's sins and short-comings than their identity in Christ?

ACTION STEPS

Taste and see that the Lord is good.
—PSALM 34:8

Instead of being quick to criticize, be quick to encourage. In doing so, you are not encouraging sin; rather, you are encouraging people to model the goodness of God. This requires you to believe the best about a person and speak to the seeds of goodness within them.

Day Twenty-five

AGREEMENT

*Behold, how good and how pleasant it is for brethren
to dwell together in unity! ...For there the Lord
commanded the blessing—life forevermore.*
—PSALM 133:1,3

There is multiplied power and effectiveness when we come together in the place of agreement. Psalm 133 reminds us that there is actually a blessing *commanded* upon unity. This is the expression of relational prosperity—a people who gather around their agreements, place their disagreements to the side, and move forward to produce change in the world. Jesus recognized the power of agreement, as He stated: *"I say to you that if two of you agree on earth concerning anything that they ask, it will be done for them by My Father in heaven. For where two or three are gathered together in My name, I am there in the midst of them"* (Matt. 18:19-20). Agreement seems to be the starting place for the impossible to come to pass in our lives. Jesus did not add qualifiers. He said that His Father *will* move on behalf of those who stand in agreement concerning *anything*.

Even those who were trying to build the Tower of Babel in Genesis 11 exhibited a measure of agreement that caught God's attention. Though their desire was wrong—believing that a structure formed by human hands could reach God—their agreement was still powerful. In fact, God responded to their efforts by observing, *"Indeed the people are one and they all have one language, and this is what they begin to do; now nothing that they propose to do will be withheld from them"* (Gen. 11:6). The key phrase being, *the people are one.* This encapsulates the essence of agreement.

Agreement is not casual or flippant. For a people to come together with the vision of building a tower into the heavens, there needed to be a strong bond of agreement gluing their efforts together. Undoubtedly, there were days when they questioned their decision. At other times, hands would get weak and legs would grow tired. There had to be the constant temptation to give up and go home on this massive building project. But not so. Though the act was frowned upon by God, the example of unity has much to teach us.

Heaven responds to our agreement on earth. As I described in the book, this demonstration of agreement is the bonding together of two hearts for or against something, issuing a "yes" or "no" on the earth that will resound in the halls of Heaven. It demands tenacity. It requires a relentless spirit. Hard times do not provoke those in agreement to give up; rather, difficulty fuels their resolve to keep pressing on in spite of opposition. The ties that bind in agreement are strong. Intimacy. Genuine concern. Love. Oneness of vision.

Just take the example of Babel and apply it to the Church. Just imagine if the Church of Jesus Christ gathered together, functioning in that dimension of unity. We would be a force on the earth that would be demolishing darkness left and right. Our "yes" and our "no" would literally shift things in the earth realm because we all stood as one in the spirit. The result of this unity is nothing short of transformational.

Relationships bound together by agreement produce change in the earth. Starting from our average, everyday decisions to influencing laws and governmental policy at a national level, agreement is a powerful force fueled by relationship. The stronger our relationships with each other, the more powerful our agreement. The more powerful our agreement, the more impossibilities will turn around and Heaven's agenda will advance in our midst.

REFLECTION QUESTIONS

Why do you think healthy relationships are important to maintaining agreement?

_____

_____

_____

_____

_____

_____

How can our agreement survive, even in the midst of opposition and difficulty, when our relationships are prosperous?

_____

_____

_____

_____

_____

_____

In what ways do you need a greater level of agreement in your current associations?

_____

_____

_____

_____

ACTION STEPS

Can two walk together, except they be agreed?
—AMOS 3:3 KJV

Consider relationships where increased unity and agreement would produce greater transformation. (In your place of work, church, volunteer work, family, etc.) Write down the top three and be intentional about cultivating unity in these contexts.

Week Six

SOCIAL PROSPERITY

You are not here merely to make a living. You are here in order to enable the world to live more amply, with greater vision, with a finer spirit of hope and achievement. You are here to enrich the world, and you impoverish yourself if you forget the errand.
—Woodrow Wilson

Day Twenty-Six

INTEGRITY

> *Remember, we Christians think man lives forever.*
> *Therefore, what really matters is those little*
> *marks or twists on the central, inside part of*
> *the soul which are going to turn it, in the long*
> *run, into a heavenly or a hellish creature.*
> —C.S. LEWIS
> *Mere Christianity*

*I*ntegrity is costly and uncommon in this world. At the same time, it positions you to walk in the *perfect will of God.* (See Romans 12:2.) How? This is what I want to explore with you today. The book gives a more clear understanding of the will of God, explaining what it means to experience the *perfect* will of God, as opposed to some more mediocre or status quo experience (which sadly, many are content to remain in).

You have been made for more than status quo. Never settle for mediocre when you have been created and redeemed to be a catalyst of transformation in your world. Remember, social change begins with soul change. Soul change happens when we understand what true integrity is and how it operates in our lives.

When we think of exemplary individuals who exhibit integrity, we consider people who live with a great degree of *oneness.* They are the same in front of an audience as they are behind closed doors—no duplicity. The pastor is the same at the pulpit as he is at the grocery store. The politician is the same person, whether delivering an impressive speech, sharing at the dinner table, or reading to the little ones at bedtime.

Integrity inspires us because it reveals the possibility of living *the same way* all the time. The world is tired of duplicity, hypocrisy, and phonies. It takes too much energy to live that way. Unfortunately, like many, we *expect* hypocrisy, and when we are exposed to integrity, we are surprised.

I want *you* to constantly surprise the world. You are a true representative and ambassador of the Kingdom of God in your sphere of influence. The Spirit of God lives within you and He enables you to live a life of integrity. Even in the midst of societal corruption and rampant immorality, you can live as a man or woman of integrity. It all begins with aligning your spirit and soul—God's thoughts directly influencing your thoughts.

Integrity is *not* perfection; it is an intentional, lifelong pursuit— it is living true to who you are and walking out your core values. Integrity begins and ends with a commitment to refuse to be anything less than what God says we are and living according to His standards. Those who don't walk in integrity won't experience God's perfect will; they will forever be content with "satisfactory" or even compromise when Heaven is calling them to greatness.

To walk in integrity, you don't have to be a spiritual superhero. Simply put, integrity is pursuing alignment between your soul and what was accomplished in your spirit because of Jesus. When you were saved/born again, your spirit was made alive. You became an entirely *new creation*. (See 2 Corinthians 5:17.) Here is the dilemma many of us face: How to allow what took place in our spirits to transform every other dimension of our being. For the sake of this teaching, we are focusing on the soul.

To experience social prosperity—where the eyes of society behold a man or woman who, every day, pursues alignment between spirit and soul—we need to begin by focusing on our thought lives. Integrity in our thought lives will ultimately produce integrity in every other realm of living.

In Romans 12:2, Paul writes concerning *renewing the mind.* What does this mean? Simple. It is your thoughts being in agreement with the thoughts of the One who has transformed your spirit. This positions you to walk in the perfect will of God. It makes complete sense. You will walk in the perfect will of God as your mind is filled with the thoughts of God. God's thoughts and method of thinking will help navigate your steps, and if your mind remains under His influence, you will walk in His ways.

REFLECTION QUESTIONS

Who can you think of who models a lifestyle of integrity? Why?

_____

_____

_____

_____

_____

Explain how you understand the connection between your spirit (specifically, the transformation that took place in your spirit at salvation) and your soul.

_____

_____

_____

_____

_____

_____

Describe what integrity in your thought life looks like.

_____

_____

_____

_____

_____

_____

ACTION STEPS

*Don't become so well-adjusted to your culture that you
fit into it without even thinking. Instead, fix your attention on God. You'll be changed from the inside out.*
—ROMANS 12:2 MSG

Today, I gave you a key place to start when it comes to walking
in God's perfect will and modeling a lifestyle of integrity—*your
mind.* How much do your thoughts reflect the thoughts of God?
This is going to be a recurring theme for this study, so don't be
surprised if you notice the topic coming up frequently. Be mindful of your mind. Too often we shrug off our thought lives and
discount them as of little consequence. In fact, what you think is
the key to the quality of life that you experience. Your thoughts
are more important than you can possibly imagine!

Day Twenty-Seven

KINGDOM-MINDEDNESS

Thy kingdom come, Thy will be done
in earth, as it is in heaven.
—MATTHEW 6:10 KJV

Today, I want to help you become so Kingdom-minded that you can't help but be of tremendous earthly good! I understand why many use the expression, "They were so heavenly minded that they were no earthly good." There is a difference between "living in the Kingdom" and the realm of Heaven. Jesus's blood made it possible for you and I to look forward to an eternity of unimaginable joy and discovery in a literal place called Heaven. To whet your appetite for this glorious eternity, I encourage you to read the Book of Revelation as well as Randy Alcorn's stunning book, *Heaven*.

Here is the problem: When you become overly mindful of one day going to Heaven, it is possible for you to become under-mindful of transforming the present world. Focusing on your future place in Heaven to the neglect of current opportunities to affect change for Christ is self-seeking—and certainly not how God intends for you to maximize your potential as a world-changer. During His life on earth, Jesus demonstrated how you should purpose to live and invest your time on this side of Heaven.

It may come as a surprise to some of us, but Jesus did not simply preach a Gospel of salvation; He preached the Gospel of the

Kingdom. Salvation is your means of entry *into* the Kingdom. Salvation is absolutely essential—there is no way to bypass the cross, it is utterly fundamental to entering into the Christian life. The disconnect happens *after* we experience salvation and live wondering, "*Now what?*" Jesus is the Door. Going beyond the Door to enjoy the fullness of Christ is what Kingdom living is all about! This is why we must teach about the Kingdom, because those of us who are heirs of salvation are now citizens of this Kingdom. Even though Heaven is a thrilling future to consider, the fact remains that we are still present on the earth.

So I must pose the question: Why isn't the body of Christ having *a greater* social impact? In times past, we have made costly trade-offs, where we upheld a "social Gospel" over a sound theology of the cross, redemption, and salvation. Even though natural ills were being addressed, the vision for the Kingdom was still absent. Our theology must incite us to action. Our revelation and grasp of what Jesus told us to pray in Matthew 6 suggests *so much more* than many of us are currently living. The good news is that *more* is available now!

As you have read, the Kingdom of God is not a topic reserved for Sunday mornings, Wednesday nights, or the occasional mission trip. The Kingdom lifestyle is not restricted to clergy, missionaries, and spiritual leaders. If you are filled with the Holy Spirit, you have been brought into the Kingdom—and you have received the *power* of the Kingdom. The Spirit of God is the One who releases the Kingdom of God *through you*. Returning to a key statement of the apostle Paul, we clearly see that the Kingdom of God is *in the Holy Spirit*. (See Romans 14:17.) Jesus was intentional about drawing a parallel between the supernatural power of the Kingdom and the Holy Spirit. (See Matthew 12:28; Luke 11:20.) When Jesus performed miracles, healed the sick, and cast out demons, the Spirit of God was moving through Him, releasing the Kingdom of God. He was proactively transforming society because He was filled with the power of the Kingdom!

Now, imagine what the Holy Spirit has made available to you! You have the same Spirit living within you that raised Jesus from the dead. (See Romans 8:11.) This means that you and I are every-day carriers of God's Kingdom. Every encounter that someone has with us is actually an encounter with the mobile Kingdom of God. No, it will not always be spectacular in demonstration. It will not always mean a miracle healing or deliverance from demonic torment. Maybe it is a simple act of kindness. Perhaps it is a word of encouragement. Never underestimate ordinary displays of God's goodness.

God's Kingdom is His order, His will, and His way of doing. This is what we are stewards of on the earth. When we understand this, our purpose to bring change to society becomes all the more clear and vivid!

REFLECTION QUESTIONS

How have you thought about the Kingdom of God in the past? Did you see it as the same thing as Heaven, or as being born again/saved?

_____

_____

_____

_____

_____

What do you think living as a citizen of God's Kingdom here on earth looks like in a practical, everyday way?

_____

_____

_____

_____

_____

_____

Describe why you think being Kingdom-minded makes you more apt to bring about societal transformation and change?

_____

_____

_____

_____

_____

ACTION STEPS

But seek (aim at and strive after) first of all
His kingdom and His righteousness (His way of
doing and being right), and then all these things
taken together will be given you besides.
—MATTHEW 6:33 AMP

Ask yourself, *"How do I put the Kingdom of God first in my everyday life? Thoughts? Decisions? Relationships?"*

Day Twenty-Eight

LEADERSHIP

Leadership is not about titles, positions, or flowcharts.
It is about one life influencing another.
—JOHN C. MAXWELL

You don't need to be recognized by your company as a partner, owner, CEO, or manager to be a leader. Leadership does not come with a title; it comes with a stewardship of your influence.

Leadership is all about how we use this thing called *influence*, and *how* we are influencing each other. It is really black and white. We are either leading people toward their purpose or away from it. We are either empowering people or disempowering them. We are either helping people fulfill what they have been called to do or promoting lifestyles of complacency. If we cannot be trusted to lead people *into* their destinies, their identities, and their callings, then we are not stewarding our influence well and will never become positioned for new levels of leadership.

Remember, leadership is not about being in charge of other people or managing people. You manage things but lead people. It not about exercising authority over everybody else while we recline comfortably "at the top." Those who idealize such a false paradigm of leadership, by definition, are not qualified for it. When it comes to stepping into new levels of influence, we must understand how God's structure of promotion works.

Who are the people God desires to promote to places of influence? Those who steward what they have already been given. These people do not despise the days of small beginnings, but they work hard, starting from the bottom, and use every opportunity as a chance to grow and develop. (See Zechariah 4:9,10.) They know how to obey in the little things, paying attention to all of the details. They are not consumed with romantic notions of being the one in charge, but instead are preoccupied with the great challenge of developing the people around them. In short, God promotes those who do their best to promote others. If you make others shine, God will make you shine.

Increase is given to *givers.* It might not make sense within our natural framework, but that's okay—we are to be Kingdom-minded. In this context, Jesus invites us to *give* and it *shall be given to us.* (See Luke 6:38.) It would appear that in Jesus's paradigm, the key to increase is giving away what we have. In other words, Jesus is looking for those who invest what they currently have in order to evaluate who qualifies for more.

Are you increasing your influence by investing in others? God is looking to invest in those who use what they have to invest in others, because He knows such people can be trusted with more.

REFLECTION QUESTIONS

How would you personally define leadership? What metaphors can you use in your description?

Why do you think the issue of stewarding your influence is so important to Jesus? How does stewardship actually position you for increase?

_____

_____

_____

_____

_____

_____

Can you think of some practical ways that you can steward your current level of influence?

_____

_____

_____

_____

_____

_____

ACTION STEPS

The key to successful leadership today
is influence, not authority.
—KEN BLANCHARD

I want you to consider where you are—*right now*. What is your job? What measure of influence have you currently been entrusted with? Just because you don't have a special title does *not* mean you are without influence. No matter what you do or where you work, you have influence. No matter who you are, you influence *someone.*

Ask yourself, *"How am I currently using my position of influence?"*

Day Twenty-Nine

SERVICE

As each one has received a special gift,
employ it in serving one another as good
stewards of the manifold grace of God.
—1 PETER 4:10 NASB

Service is yet another expression of stewardship and the key to greatness. (See Matthew 23:11.) God wants you to experience greater development, growth, and maturity in your gifting. However, the test for whether we are qualified for increase is one of stewardship. It means that we take the gifts that God has given to us *seriously*. We do this through service. A day has to come when we identify what God has placed within us and recognize that this grace is not exclusively for our benefit.

I think of Jesus's Parable of the Talents as the ultimate blueprint for God's method of determining who was *faithful* with the gifting entrusted to them, and who was a poor steward of the Master's grace. There are many ways we could approach this incredible story, but I want to focus on the first two verses. It is here where the servants are summoned into their stewardship. Let's start at the beginning and remain there:

> *For it will be like a man going on a journey, who called*
> *his servants and entrusted to them his property. To one*

*he gave five talents, to another two, to another one, to
each according to his ability. Then he went away.*
—MATTHEW 25:14-15 ESV

Let's reflect on the following points that Jesus raises through this parable:

1. *We are stewards.* The men who are given the talents are recognized, first and foremost, as stewards. Likewise, this is one of our principle identities before the Lord. Just because we enjoy intimacy and friendship with God, this does not negate the fact that we are also His stewards. Friendship does not cancel out our responsibility before the Lord; it fuels it. We serve One whom we know, love, and desire to honor with our lives. So, as His stewards, what do we do? We use what we have been given to serve others.

2. *We receive gifts from the Master because of grace.* Before we look at *how much* each servant is given, I want you to note that the man calls his servants together and *entrusts to them his property.* The master takes the first step by identifying these men as his chosen servants. In other words, the master is the one who turns these men into his stewards. He gives them this title and its corresponding duties by his grace—his decision. It is not based on their merit, but rather, his plan. God operates the same way with you and me. We receive gifts, not based on who we are or what we do, but on who He is and according to the plans He wants to release into the earth through us.

3. *We are increased according to faithfulness.*[1] Every servant was given *something.* Their gift is multiplied because of their faithfulness to wisely steward what the master had given them. One of the key ways that we wisely steward the gifts and graces that the Lord has entrusted to us is through serving others. Truly, this yields a bountiful, multiplied harvest!

REFLECTION QUESTIONS

Read the Parable of the Talents in Matthew 25:14-30. Why is it so important that we know who God really is if we are going to steward our gifts effectively? (Consider the wicked servant and his response to the Master in verses 24-30.)

_____

_____

_____

_____

_____

_____

In what ways can you position yourself for growth, development, and increase in your giftings?

_____

_____

_____

_____

_____

ACTION STEPS

To serve God is the deliberate love-gift of a
nature that has heard the call of God.
—OSWALD CHAMBERS[2]

Your service is actually _worship_ before the Lord. You are responding to who God is by what you do through these acts. We don't serve to gain God's approval. No. We serve because we _have_

God's approval through Christ and our desire is to reflect this gratitude day and night.

In truth, our service reveals *how* we view God. Remember the wicked and lazy servant in Matthew 25? His service suffered because he had a poor view of the master. However, when we know who our God is—His love, His compassion, His goodness— we serve people in response to these attributes. In fact, we want to *serve* these attributes to people through our lives because we desire for all to experience the God we know.

1. See Luke 19:17.

2. Oswald Chambers, *My Utmost for His Highest* (Uhrichsville, OH: Barbour Publishing, 1935), January 17.

Day Thirty

JUSTICE

*I would like to be known as a person who is
concerned about freedom and equality and
justice and prosperity for all people.*
—ROSA PARKS

There are many hearts around the world that are crying out for justice. Remember, all of humanity was created in the image and likeness of God. This means that there are certain innate qualities we all exhibit that unveil certain attributes of our Creator. One such characteristic is the desire for justice. The Creator of the Universe is the ultimate Just Judge.

Both in and outside of the Church, there has been a significant movement toward social justice causes. This is worth celebrating. At the same time, I believe God wants to upgrade your vision for what true justice is and what it is designed to produce in someone's life.

Christianity actually invites you into a revolutionary expression of justice. Yes, you are to remain focused on helping alleviate the assorted natural ills that are plaguing the world—from the epidemic of poverty to the devastation of disease to the horrors of sex trafficking. We focus on bringing hope in the midst of these atrocities, practically and spiritually. At times, one might look at how the Church and the world approach the issue of social justice and wonder, "What is the difference?"

Here's the difference: Not only do we desire to alleviate the immediate problem, but we also desire to bring every man, woman, boy, and girl into a safe, loving relationship with the Perfect Father. The Vindicator. The Healer. The Redeemer. The Deliverer. We bring natural and spiritual solutions. I am ever amazed at how our God reveals Himself to whomever or however the situation needs Him to be manifested. Justice is not simply an act; it is a Person. When we become emissaries of justice, we are stepping into our identities as those created in the image of the God of justice.

Jesus Himself declared that He came "*to set at liberty those who are oppressed*" (Luke 4:18). If anyone personified the heart of God to remedy injustice on the planet, it was the Person of Jesus Christ.

You might look at Him and think to yourself, "Yes, but that was Jesus."

Don't let the call for justice overwhelm you. It begins in the ordinary, mundane trenches of everyday life. It is your call to help your neighbors, stand up for the homeless, and represent the dignity of every human being.

You might be asking, "Where do I start?" Without a doubt, the injustices running rampant in the world are overwhelming. The wonderful truth is that your starting place is a position of great power and effectiveness—*your voice before the courts of Heaven*. The blood of Jesus has given you bold access before the throne of grace to raise your voice and intercede on behalf of the voiceless.

When intercession is coupled with action, you become the most powerful force on earth. Not all are called to the front lines—but there is a place for you in the halls of prayer. Just ask the Lord how you can put action to your prayers in any of these causes.

REFLECTION QUESTIONS

How do you think our desire for justice models the character and nature of God?

_____

_____

_____

_____

_____

_____

What does Jesus reveal about God's heart toward injustice?

_____

_____

_____

_____

_____

Read Hebrews 4:16. How is your voice a powerful weapon against injustice?

_____

_____

_____

_____

_____

_____

ACTION STEPS

Let us therefore come boldly to the throne of grace, that we
may obtain mercy and find grace to help in time of need.
—HEBREWS 4:16

Begin in the place of prayer. This is where the Lord will give you a strategy for how you can meet needs in practical, everyday ways. Perhaps there is a cause that burns in your heart—pray about ways to get more involved. Do your research. Now is the time to take a stand for justice. *This* is how you experience the *richer life.* "It is by spending myself that I become rich," said the legendary Sarah Bernhardt. When you play even a small role in bringing a remedy to the suffering of humanity, you are giving expression to what Jesus described as the *abundant life.* (See John 10:10.) What the thief has stolen or destroyed, you are coming against with life, hope, and healing.

Week Seven

VOCATIONAL PROSPERITY

Don't aim at success. The more you aim at it and make it a target, the more you are going to miss it. For success, like happiness, cannot be pursued; it must ensue, and it only does so as the unintended side effect of one's personal dedication to a cause greater than oneself or as the by-product of one's surrender to a person other than oneself.
—Viktor Frankl
Man's Search for Meaning

Day Thirty-One

PURPOSE

*Therefore do not be ashamed of the testimony of our Lord,
nor of me His prisoner, but share with me in the sufferings
for the gospel according to the power of God, who has
saved us and called us with a holy calling, not according
to our works, but according to His own purpose and grace
which was given to us in Christ Jesus before time began.*
—2 TIMOTHY 1:8-9

God is sovereign and strategic—He has marvelous plans set in place for you—yet you are responsible to walk in step with His Spirit in order to fulfill the purpose and calling on your life. You have been invited to participate in the unfolding of your purpose. Whether or not you fully grasp what that is in the present moment, I invite you to shift your life out of neutral and put your purpose into gear. How? By keeping step with the Spirit—knowing His rhythm and pace for your life. Don't try to run someone else's race, because God has a race to run for you. Keep pace with God.

The apostle Paul reminds us to walk in the Spirit. In Galatians 5:25, he writes, "*Since we live by the Spirit, let us keep in step with the Spirit*" (NIV). This is the key to fulfilling your purpose and walking out your destiny. It is not mysterious, magical, or mystical. It is simply cooperating with the Holy Spirit even when you don't fully comprehend the outcome—leaning not on your own understanding (see Ps. 3:5), but saying "yes" at every opportunity.

Some act as if the prize of fulfilling purpose is given only to a select few, while everyone else is doomed to wander through life aimlessly. Purpose is not assigned to an elect group. Every single person throughout history was created with precision and intentionality by the Master Creator. Every human being has a purpose. Here is the question: *"Are you walking in step with the Spirit to discover yours and to manifest it in your daily life?"*

God is the only One who can lead you into His perfect plan for your life. We have studied this in part, reading about how renewing your mind fills you with the thoughts of God. When God's thoughts become your thoughts, you begin to think about your life *like God does*—enabling you to walk out *His* great destiny for you.

It is one thing to replace old paradigms, thought patterns, and deceptions with the truth of God's Word (the Bible reveals the thought patterns of God). It is another thing to start *living* by the thoughts of God. This is what Paul was telling the Galatian church. He was calling them to a new level of alignment. Because we have been born again and redeemed by the Holy Spirit, filled with His presence, we must begin to walk in step—or in alignment—with this reality. This means allowing the Spirit of God to have control in every area of your life. You can sing "I Surrender All" with great passion while still holding back select areas of your life from God's direct influence.

Many wrestle with surrendering their calling to God because they do not believe it is a *holy calling.* One is not *called* only if he or she dons a church or ministry title. Your calling in the marketplace, medical field, law, entertainment industry, or educational sphere is just as sacred as the pastor's call to lead a church. God desires you to represent Him in every arena of society. To do this, you must embrace a paradigm of *holy calling* that sees *all* mediums of vocation as sacred.

The key to fulfilling your unique calling in whatever sphere of influence God has equipped you for is an active relationship with the Holy Spirit.

REFLECTION QUESTIONS

What is the danger of thinking that only people in full-time ministry (pastors, missionaries, evangelists, priests, rabbis, etc.) are fulfilling a *holy calling*?

Describe what you think it looks like to live "*in step with the Spirit*" based on what Paul writes in Galatians 5:25; look up different translations of this verse for further clarity.

Explain how fulfilling your purpose/destiny is a collaboration between you and the Holy Spirit.

_____

_____

_____

_____

ACTION STEPS

He who has a why to live for can bear almost any how.
—FRIEDRICH NIETZSCHE

Ask the Lord to give you clarity on the one simple step you can take to fulfill your holy calling and divine purpose right now! Remember, the key to making progress in your life is making one step a day. By the year's end, you will have made 365 steps toward fulfilling your destiny!

Day Thirty-Two

DILIGENCE

What we hope ever to do with ease, we
must first learn to do with diligence.
—SAMUEL JOHNSON

Diligence begins with recognizing this: *The sum of the small is what creates the large.* Every decision fueled by diligence is the difference between ordinary and extraordinary. It has weight. It plays into the unfolding of a greater purpose, plan, or vision. Through it you are able to deliver the "wow" rather than the "whoa."

There are great rewards for your diligence. In addition to positioning you for favor, you will gain and sustain a sense of fulfillment. Excellence will become the signature of your work. You will exemplify standout performance on the job. In *The Prosperous Soul* book, I explain in detail how diligence is expressed: To be diligent is to dot every "i" and cross every "t." It is being thorough, doing things right the first time, and stopping to think of the things no one else has taken the time to consider. It is taking care of relationships while at the same time getting the job done, and not at the expense of one thing over the other. It is to hold customers with a high regard while also cherishing your employees. Once again, it embraces the practice of wholeness rather than lock-step priorities.

The key to practicing diligence is having a clear vision of your desired future results. This does not mean having every detail of your work or endeavor planned out. The Holy Spirit often gives only the broad strokes of a vision, dream, or image—sometimes just a word, phrase, or idea. That's it. And yet, that's not it.

Diligence is the key to unlocking visions and dreams for your future. It is your way of collaborating with the Holy Spirit to bring your purpose to pass. The truth is, the One who knows every angle of every possibility and outcome lives within you. The Holy Spirit—the One who guides you into all truth and shows you things to come—is the most trustworthy of companions. When He gives you a brief snapshot of the future, He is not taunting you or playing games with your mind. He is drawing you into a place of hunger and dependency—because when you get a glimpse of the magnitude of what He is calling you into, it reminds you of your complete dependency upon Him.

The Holy Spirit empowers you to be diligent. The power source of Heaven is within you. He not only enables you to perform great supernatural exploits, but also strengthens you in the everyday decisions of diligence. Keep in mind that your simple steps of diligence are monumental strides toward walking out your destiny.

You do not wake up into your destiny. No. You walk into it. You step into it. Everything to do regarding your purpose and destiny demands movement. To get to the next level, you must move forward. How do you demonstrate eligibility for the next level? With diligence.

Joseph's diligence in Potiphar's house, and then in prison, proved he was eligible to rule over Egypt alongside Pharaoh. He was given a glimpse of a glorious destiny through a dream—and then, the dreamer was diligent in every season and circumstance.

Prosperity is clothed in diligence. As a result of diligence, Joseph's dream became a reality. He was able to fulfill his purpose and leave an indelible mark on history.

Become a history maker through diligence.

REFLECTION QUESTIONS

Why do you think diligence is so important to stepping into destiny?

_____

_____

_____

_____

_____

_____

What are some practical ways that you can be diligent *where you are* in order to get where you *want to be* in your job?

_____

_____

_____

_____

_____

_____

How is Joseph an example of the way diligence positions you to fulfill your dreams?

_____

_____

_____

_____

_____

_____

ACTION STEPS

He who has a slack hand becomes poor, but
the hand of the diligent makes rich.
—PROVERBS 10:4

Diligence positions you to fulfill your destiny. This means that you have an essential part to play in fulfilling God's plan for your life. Simply ask, *"What part do You want me to play today, Lord?"*

Day Thirty-Three

INVESTMENT

I press on toward the goal to win the prize for which
God has called me heavenward in Christ Jesus.
—**PHILIPPIANS** 3:14 NIV

There is no significant return without a wise investment. Correspondingly, the level of your investment in the things of the spirit determines the level of the return you receive. (See Galatians 6:8-9.)

Investment is *not* just about finances. As I described in *The Prosperous Soul* book, there are three key things you can choose to spend, waste, or invest: Your time, your talents, and your treasure. To experience richness in each of these areas, you need to understand *how* to make wise investments.

We are used to spending money, spending time, and spending our talents. Every interaction and activity of your day, however, is an opportunity for investment. Rather than spend time, invest it. Realize that once a resource is spent—whether time, energy, or an opportunity—it's gone, it's wasted. If instead you intentionally invest your assets, you will see a compound—even exponential—return.

What we offer the world is extremely valuable. The problem is that many of us are wasting the very commodities that, if invested, could make a significant difference in the lives of those closest to us, and for those we regularly encounter in our spheres of influence.

You are probably wondering, *What does it look like to invest the intangibles of talent and time?* The starting place is wisdom. You cannot be idle when it comes to the resources you have been entrusted with. You must learn the art of evaluating, asking yourself, "Is this a good investment, or is it the *best* investment?" *Good* often invites you to receive an instant return, while *best* might yield results you won't see until sometime in the future. *Best* is always the option that produces the richest long-term return.

If you want to experience a richer life, learn to invest. It is the wise investors who reap a multiplicity of returns. Become a wise investor of your time, treasure, and talent—and experience a multiplied return in every area of your life.

You must never underestimate the power you have to invest in the precious moments of your days, for what remains at the end of the day you will have invested a portion of your life for it. Take time to restore, refuel, and refresh regularly—it's an investment that will energize you to be more active and invested in every other area of your life.

Start evaluating everything you do by this simple question: "Is this a *good* decision that will *spend* my time/talent/treasure, or is this the *best* decision that will *invest* my time/talent/treasure?"

REFLECTION QUESTIONS

Describe your understanding of the practice of *investment*. How does it help you to see your time, talent, and treasures differently?

In what ways can an investment-minded person experience increase in their time and talent? (It is easy to wrap our minds around financial investments producing increase; I want to help you see how other investments produce a different kind of increase.)

_____

_____

_____

_____

_____

_____

Pick one area of your life where you would like to see a greater return on investment. Evaluate how you are currently stewarding this area.

_____

_____

_____

_____

_____

_____

ACTION STEPS

Sentiment without action is the ruin of the soul.
—EDWARD ABBEY

I want you to enjoy a multiplied return on investment in every area of your life! The key is identifying where you are *not* making the best investments and start changing the way you steward your time, talent, and treasures. Ask yourself, *"Where do I need to make better investments in life?*" Remember, God qualifies us for increase based on stewardship. Investment demonstrates that we can be trusted with more, rather than being someone who simply wastes or squanders what he or she has been given for a quick result.

Day Thirty-four

GOOD WORK

Your work is going to fill a large part of your life, and
the only way to be truly satisfied is to do...great work.
—STEVE JOBS

*N*ever underestimate the prospering power of good work. Doing good work is not a drudgery to be endured—it is actually a gift from God! In *The Prosperous Soul* book, I provide a basic overview of what good work looks like and, specifically, how you can experience richness in each of the eight realms of life through your job.

Today, I want to help you see your job as a vehicle for holistic prosperity. I have given you a blueprint for what your career should be. However, I am sure that, after reading through the chapter in the book, you might be thinking to yourself, "I don't feel that way about my current job," or, "I will feel that way *when* I have my dream career." Let's address the nuts and bolts of how to enjoy richness, day after day, in a job that might not be ideal.

The fact is, you can actually enjoy good work even when you are working at a job that might not be your definition of perfect. How so? By maintaining a *prosperity perspective*. In an age where everything trains us to be negative, fault-finding, dissatisfied, and hyper-critical, learn to go against the flow. Start with your job. If it's not ideal, you can still make some ideal choices. This entire week has been focused on practical keys that will help you enjoy prosperity in your present vocation while also positioning you for future promotion.

In order to be positioned for increased future success, you must enjoy where you *are* on the way to where you are headed. Prosperity was never meant to begin *then*; it is available right now. The only reason we limit prosperity to a future date (when we get that "one thing" or "one break" we are hoping for) is because we have embraced a limited definition of the word. It's not as much about what we get out of our work as it is what we put into it. Prosperity is not living with the absence of struggles or problems—but embracing them with the passion that drives us to do good work. If you are waiting to do "good work" for when you are in your "perfect job," you will never position yourself for prosperity.

Doing good work is not about a job. It's about being fully present and committed to the good that can come from the work at hand—combining the principles of diligence and investment, being purpose-driven in every given moment. God will prosper *every* work you set your hands to when you approach it from a prosperity perspective—making all work good work. Your work is your signature—shoddy or excellent, either way it testifies of who you are as a person.

Honor God in all the work you do, however frustrating, discouraging, or thankless it may seem. God will promote you in due time if you are faithful *in doing good*. (See Galatians 6:9.) It is all about embracing the right perspective and working out of that place. You can always do good work—even great work—because, at the end of the day, you know that you are ultimately working for God.

REFLECTION QUESTIONS

Consider your current job/place of employment. What is your perspective about where you work? What about the work that you do?

_____

_____

_____

_____

_____

Based on today's lesson, why do you think it is important to have a *prosperity perspective* on your job?

_____

_____

_____

_____

_____

Write out some practical decisions that you can start making on how you can change the way you approach your job. (Even though it may not be your dream job, you can still prosper where you *are* on the way to where you are *headed*. Prosperity begins with your perspective and attitude of heart.)

_____

_____

_____

_____

_____

_____

ACTION STEPS

*Take care of yourself, have a good time, and make the
most of whatever job you have for as long as God gives
you life. And that's about it. That's the human lot. Yes,
we should make the most of what God gives, both the
bounty and the capacity to enjoy it, accepting what's
given and delighting in the work. It's God's gift!*
—ECCLESIASTES 5:18-19 MSG

Good work begins with an attitude, not an ideal scenario or
circumstances. You can enjoy prosperity in your career *right now*
simply by changing the way you approach your job. You may
not be in your dream career, but you can position yourself for
increased success by the quality of work you do today.

Day Thirty-five

HOLY AMBITION

*Not that I have already attained, or am already perfected;
but I press on, that I may lay hold of that for which Christ
Jesus has also laid hold of me. Brethren, I do not count
myself to have apprehended; but one thing I do, forgetting
those things which are behind and reaching forward to
those things which are ahead, I press toward the goal
for the prize of the upward call of God in Christ Jesus.*
PHILIPPIANS 3:12-14

*I*f anyone exhibited holy, sanctified ambition, it was the apostle Paul. When we talk about the concept of "ambition," there are negative stigmas often attached. This is not because ambition, in and of itself, is a bad thing. Unfortunately, people have used it as a vehicle for ungodly pursuits. A driving ambition for the wrong things has consistently been responsible for jeopardizing other realms of life. If any type of ambition displaces other important realms of life—such as our faith, family, or friendships—then the ambition is misplaced. Ambition is extremely powerful, for both good and for bad. What is your intention and motive for doing something?

Paul was intimately acquainted with this. He lived on both sides of ambition. Before his Damascus Road encounter with Christ, Paul was feared among the Christian community because of his ungodly ambition. He was the great persecutor of the Church, *not* the impassioned evangelist of the lost. He was zealous to destroy, not build up. All of this would change after one encounter in the presence of the Risen Christ.

Ambition should be measured in God's presence. In any given moment, you can pause to prayerfully ask yourself, *"Does the fulfillment of my ambition extend glory to God?"* It demands a moment-by-moment heart check to test whether your present drive—whatever it may be—is glorifying to God.

Your greatest source of delight and ultimate fulfillment should be giving God glory. This is not some rote, religious response. It is not duty or obligation. You delight in giving God glory, and likewise, He invites you to partake in His glory. To give God glory is the greatest source of human fulfillment imaginable. This is the true sweet spot of living out of our created purpose and design. Everyone wants to know the meaning of life, right? The *Westminster Confession of Faith* captures it aptly: "The chief end of man is to glorify God and enjoy Him forever." I am continually amazed at how God brings us such enjoyment when we are able to give Him glory.

Be assured, holy ambition is no "church exclusive" passion. You give God glory by being the man or woman He put you on this planet to be. You give God glory by fulfilling your designated assignment in whatever unique sphere of influence you have been stationed. You experience great fulfillment and satisfaction when you *do* things that give God glory. I am amazed at how the things that give God glory are also the things that make us come fully alive. It is truly the goodness of our loving God to allow for so great an intersection between our passion and His glory.

Whether it's teaching, singing, writing, acting, practicing medicine, or upholding the law, when you do *everything* as you are doing it unto God, you are giving Him glory. When you invest your talents in good soil, you give God glory. When you receive payoff on the investments that you make, you give God glory.

To give God the glory that is due His name, you are not simply attending a worship service—you are living a worship lifestyle. Your ambition, regardless of what field, specialty, or trade it finds fulfillment in—if it's Heaven-birthed and stands the testing of God's presence—is meant to give God glory. Celebrate where you are and what you are doing, knowing that you have the ability to glorify God in every moment.

REFLECTION QUESTIONS

What are some practical ways that you can measure your ambition in God's presence? (Prayer, worship, dialogue with the Holy Spirit, etc.)

_____

_____

_____

_____

_____

List some signs of what you think *unholy* ambition looks like. (This will be helpful to you in evaluating your own ambition; it is important to know what the negative looks like so you can recognize and avoid it.)

_____

_____

_____

_____

_____

_____

How can your personal ambitions bring God glory? Explain.

_____

_____

_____

_____

_____

_____

ACTION STEPS

So whether you eat or drink or whatever
you do, do it all for the glory of God.
—1 CORINTHIANS 10:31 NIV

I want you to discover how what you are *currently doing* can bring glory to God. Too many of us are waiting for some supernatural "call to ministry," when in fact, where we currently are positioned is a call to ministry in and of itself. What you are doing, the people you work with every day, and the job you are responsible for doing with excellence—this is not simply your place of employment, but is a holy place of worship. Your work, when done from this perspective, is actually a form of worship to the praise and glory of God.

Week Eight

FINANCIAL PROSPERITY

*God can pour on the blessings in astonishing ways
so that you're ready for anything and everything,
more than just ready to do what needs to be done.*
—2 Corinthians 9:8 msg

ENOUGH

Content people don't always have the best of everything,
but they always make the best of everything.
—DAVE RAMSEY

When is enough enough? *Enough* is the result of the right kind of attitude that we embrace concerning money. Paul made it clear that godliness *with* contentment is the source of the greatest gain. (See 1 Timothy 6:6.) He did not say that the greatest gain is having the most money in the bank.

In this quest to experience prosperity in every realm of life, you are now coming to the end of your journey. I have placed *financial prosperity* last, not because God is not concerned about it; He definitely is. However, so many have entertained such a skewed perspective on prosperity that we need to review it in context. If every other realm of your life is broken, and yet you still pursue financial increase, you are out of balance. Prosperity in the true biblical sense is so much more than money—it is wholeness in every area of life. This is why we have been exploring eight key areas that a prosperous soul directly impacts. Financial prosperity is only one of them.

There are those who serve money, and then there are those whose money serves them. Rich, poor—doesn't matter. Anyone can be in bondage to the pursuit of financial gain. The person living in financial lack lives hand to mouth, needing to get up every morning to go to work for fear that without that week's work hours, food wouldn't be on the table, rent wouldn't be paid, the kids wouldn't have school supplies, and the like—and that's not even considering putting money away for college, retirement, or those big purchases we would all love to make, from new furniture to a new car.

Likewise, the one in bondage to money can also appear to be the model of success, but in fact has leveraged their credit to the maximum. They have a wonderful big house with a mortgage they can't afford. They have nice cars that the bank owns. They pay for everything on credit cards, hoping to catch up on last month's groceries with this month's paycheck.

And there are those who have bank accounts overflowing, who could write a check for a new home if they wanted to, but they just don't feel they are secure enough. All of these people, whether in lack or abundance, have no peace or contentment when it comes to financial matters. No matter what they do, they will never have enough.

Enough is an attitude. It is the result of the person who sees money for what it is—a tool, not a goal. They recognize that money by itself is not good and it is not bad; money is a method. It is a means to accomplish something. It is a currency for making a transaction. When we start to see money as more than what it truly is, we have perverted our understanding of its purpose. This is what drags us into the place of bondage.

Life is not about acquiring more money; it is about enjoying what we have and celebrating the increase along the way. Contentment is a powerful attitude, for it keeps us out of financial bondage. Our ultimate Source of trust is Jehovah Jireh—*the Lord whose provision shall be seen*—not a dollar amount.

Contentment does *not* mean that pursuing success in life is bad. Not at all. It just means that you do not idolize success, and that your definition of success is very different from the world's.

REFLECTION QUESTIONS

In what ways can the pursuit of more (more money, more possessions, etc.) put people into a place of bondage?

_____

_____

_____

_____

_____

Ask the Holy Spirit to help you honestly evaluate your own heart. Are you living a content, grateful life? Or, do you find yourself being drawn into the system of the world that emphasizes acquiring and pursuing more?

_____

_____

_____

_____

God is *not* against you pursuing success; He is the God of increase and promotion! Why do you think that it is so important to live a thankful, grateful life if you are going to pursue greater success—and not fall into a place of bondage?

_____

_____

_____

_____

_____

_____

ACTION STEPS

Now godliness with contentment is great gain.
—1 TIMOTHY 6:6

Think of some ways you can practice contentment in your life today. This is how you live from an *enough* perspective. This may take a few minutes, as society trains us to always be looking to acquire more. Even though success is not evil, to live in bondage to the idea that "more equals contentment" is to believe a lie. I want to help you root out any lies you may be believing about contentment and enjoy where you are and what you have.

TRUSTEESHIP

He who is faithful in what is least is faithful also
in much; and he who is unjust in what is least
is unjust also in much. Therefore if you have not
been faithful in the unrighteous mammon, who
will commit to your trust the true riches?
—LUKE 16:10-11

We have been exploring this underlying topic of trusteeship throughout our entire journey together. You could also call it stewardship. In the same measure that God stewards you with gifts, talents, and favor, He entrusts you with finances. It is prosperity with purpose and money with meaning. Your level of trustworthiness with what you are presently being given determines your qualification for increase.

To be a trustee is to manage assets on behalf of another. What they manage must be used to fund various projects, endeavors, or institutions as specified by the true owner of the trust. The older term for this, which is more frequently used in the Church, is "stewardship." It is a term, however, that has lost much of its meaning. We have used the language of financial stewardship so much in the Church world that we have limited our understanding of its greater scope and purpose. It is *not* exclusive to giving tithes and offerings at church—this is merely one expression of it.

In fact, stewardship and trusteeship is not *just* about giving. It is about *ownership*.

The place where we get into trouble is when we give a certain percentage—let's say ten percent—and then assume the other ninety percent is ours to spend as we would like. That is a misperception. You see, *we don't own any of it*. It *all* belongs to God. Scripture reinforces this consistently. (See Psalm 50:10; Haggai 2:8.) As such, we are *trustees* of the finances that flow through our hands, and if we are spending everything on ourselves, we are taking the "trust" out of "trusteeship." We need to elevate our understanding of what trusteeship looks like in order to walk in true financial prosperity. In the book, I give you a picture of how to appropriately view the remaining 90 percent of your finances, and how that amount should specifically be allocated.

In order to embrace this ownership shift—that *all of it* belongs to God—I want to give you a very encouraging visual. I heard one leader present it this way: It is living with your hands open. In this state, there is a constant flow—in and out. Finances come in, and they go out. And yet, once they go out, they come back in again. Likewise, when your fists are tightly clenched around what you perceive to be *yours*, you are unable to receive (and thus, release) the increase. Ownership opens your hands for greater levels of increase and prosperity than you can imagine. The key is living as though *none* of it is yours and that *all* of it is God's property.

Jesus makes the issue of trusteeship very clear in Luke 16. There is something about *how* we can be trusted with finances (which Jesus calls "unrighteous mammon") that positions us to experience increase, not only financially but also, more importantly, in what are *true riches*. This intrigues and inspires me. I want to empower you to be a person God can trust with His *true riches*. So where do you begin?

Simple. Commit *everything* to God, recognizing that He owns it all—not just the percent that goes to a church or ministry. And live with hands open, always ready to receive and release the supernatural prosperity that you are entrusted with.

REFLECTION QUESTIONS

How do you understand financial stewardship?

_____

_____

_____

_____

_____

In what ways does your perspective of money change when you realize that God _owns everything_?

_____

_____

_____

_____

_____

What does it look like to you to live with "hands open"?

_____

_____

_____

_____

_____

ACTION STEPS

*Abundance isn't God's provision for me to live in
luxury. It's His provision for me to help others live. God
entrusts me with His money not to build my kingdom
on earth, but to build His Kingdom in heaven.*
—RANDY ALCORN

Get ready to change the way you see money, prosperity, and increase. I want to help you live as a representative of God's Kingdom, with hands open before the Giver of all good things. Remember, He wants to release finances for you to *receive* in order for you to release them again. How are you currently living? Are your hands closed or open when it comes to the finances you are receiving?

STOREHOUSES

*Here's a scary thought: What if God called you
to give beyond your comfort level? Would you be
afraid? Would you try to explain it away or dismiss
it as impractical? And in the process, would you
miss out on a harvest opportunity for which God
had explicitly prospered you in the first place?*
—ANDY STANLEY

To enjoy *true* financial prosperity, both now and in a sustained measure later in life, you must embrace saving money. Though many view saving negatively, I assure you, I'm not suggesting you never buy a new car, new clothes, or take vacations. The key is saving with a vision to purchase these things from a place of abundance and not of lack.

Today's chapter in *The Prosperous Soul* book explained the biblical significance of storehouses and the powerful imagery they convey to us today. I am convinced that in order to walk in the measures of prosperity God wants to release, you *must* grasp this subject as vitally important. You need to have a vision for saving that allows you to harness the power of supernatural blessing. (See Deuteronomy 28:8.)

The Israelites were accustomed to living with at least three storehouses of grain at all times. This was the responsible way to live—with two or three years of income stored away to cover their needs. To have less was foolhardy; to have more was unnecessary. Two to three years of reserves was all the grain they needed at all times, unless there were catastrophic problems like multiple years of drought, war, or famine. Wisdom dictated they have at least three storehouses—faith and their relationship to God would take care of the rest.

A storehouse mentality will protect you from spending when you don't have the money to spend. In Israel's context, storehouses set very clear limits. There was only so much grain in the storehouses. Once it was empty, there was no more. This is most certainly *not* the perspective of society today. When we are running on empty, we fall back on credit cards, loans, and other means of spending money that we do not possess in our storehouse.

Unfortunately, when this becomes your approach to finances, what comes into the storehouse is immediately spoken for. It has *already* been spent and needs to be directed toward debt. This is why I encouraged you about the necessity of budgeting. When you do not set clear parameters for the dispersion of finances, it becomes easy to spend money that is not available. Alternatively, when the money in that category is gone, you stop spending until you have replenished the account. This is how you embrace the storehouse principle in your everyday relationship with money.

For additional resources on these topics, I would recommend any of the materials by Dave Ramsey or Larry Burkett. They provide some excellent examples of how to practically manage your finances, regardless of the level of debt you have incurred or financial irresponsibility you have dealt with.

I want to take this moment to encourage you—you are not beyond God's grace in this! The worst lie you can believe when it comes to overcoming poor stewardship is this: *"You can't get out of this."* The testimonies are endless of people who decided to embrace a "storehouse" approach concerning the allocation of finances—and went on to experience incredible victory, despite their horrible starting conditions. Don't allow your current financial state to keep you from moving forward. Change begins by taking the first step. You will be glad you did!

REFLECTION QUESTIONS

How do you understand the *storehouse* concept of financial saving and allocation?

_____

_____

_____

_____

_____

List some benefits of embracing a financial *storehouse* system:

_____

_____

_____

_____

_____

Evaluate your current financial state. You might be adhering to the *storehouse* system right now (although you don't use that particular title to describe it). Maybe you're not, and you've incurred debt as a result. Think about where you currently are and write down your vision for where you would like to be:

_____

_____

_____

ACTION STEPS

The Lord will command the blessing on you
in your storehouses and in all to which you set
your hand, and He will bless you in the land
which the Lord your God is giving you.
—DEUTERONOMY 28:8

I hope that you have a clear picture of where you currently are financially and have a vision for where you would like to be. I encourage you to get specific here. Surely, all of us desire to be financially stable and successful. Get a little more detailed. I want you to develop a vision for how you plan to practice the storehouse principle in your life and in the finances that have been entrusted to your care.

Day Thirty-Nine

THE JOSEPH PRINCIPLE

For whoever has, to him more will be given, and he
will have abundance; but whoever does not have,
even what he has will be taken away from him.
—MATTHEW 13:12

To put the *Joseph Principle* to work, you are taking a step beyond what is typically accepted financial behavior and catapulting yourself into the *extraordinary*. This is what I want to talk about today—how to have an extraordinary spirit. This is the foundation for practicing the *Joseph Principle* in your life. More than a formula, it is a perspective. If you can operate in the extraordinary wisdom that God has made available to you, making unusual decisions while everyone else is going with the "flow," you not only position yourself for prosperity, but you can also become a place of refuge and blessing to others who are experiencing difficulty in their lives.

In short, to practice the *Joseph Principle* means to save when everyone else is spending. Living by this principle is operating from a place of godly wisdom where you are able to discern *when* to save, *how much* to save, and *what* to specifically invest in.

In Genesis 41:33, we see the qualities of one who practices the *Joseph Principle*: "*So, Pharaoh needs to look for a wise and experienced man and put him in charge of the country*" (MSG). Pay attention to the description of the person Pharaoh is seeking—one who is wise and experienced. Other translations use the word *discerning.* Joseph's wisdom prepared Egypt for both the prosperous times and the hard times that were soon to come.

As we notice in the life of Joseph, he implemented a strategy that ultimately saved Egypt's economy during a time of great famine. This wisdom not only spared Egypt, but also elevated it to become a world superpower. Egypt became a shade tree that others could take refuge under during the time of famine. This is what brought Joseph's family to the land and ultimately led to their memorable reconciliation.

Let's take this beyond money for a moment. You will only manage your money to the degree that you embrace this principle in every area of your life. Joseph received divine dreams, but he also experienced significant opposition. He was called by God to accomplish extraordinary things, but he also *positioned* himself for promotion. The key was his extraordinary spirit. For Joseph, it was all about attitude, perseverance, and excellence.

From being thrown into the pit by his own flesh and blood (and sold into slavery), to being falsely accused of rape by Potiphar's wife, to being locked up in prison, Joseph kept himself positioned for promotion. Circumstances did not determine his attitude. Rather, his attitude and perspective were what kept him bouncing back. He never gave in to self-pity, discouragement, or despair. No doubt he struggled with such things. It would be foolish to believe otherwise, considering his circumstances. However, *something* kept positioning Joseph for breakthrough, even in the midst of pits and prisons. I want you to possess what Joseph had so you can experience prosperity in every realm of your life.

Let's end by considering Joseph's time in prison. Rather than surrendering to the circumstances at hand, believing that prison bars would become his lifelong view and that the dreams God had given him would die with him in the dungeon, he exemplified a *different* spirit. In the midst of his imprisonment, Joseph was willing to be a blessing to others. He continued to steward his gifts, even when he could not see the full picture. He continued to be a man of excellence, even when his surroundings were horrific. *This is unusual* and I believe that for you to experience *unusual prosperity* you must resolve to be an *unusual person*. You make unusual decisions. You steward finances unusually when measured next to how friends, family, and the rest of society is treating money.

Remember, extraordinary decisions give birth to extraordinary results! Be okay with being *unusual* and trust God's wisdom when it comes to stewarding finances. Today, according to 3 John 2, I wish above all things that you may prosper and be in good health even as your soul prospers!

REFLECTION QUESTIONS

What do you think it means to have an *unusual* or *extraordinary* spirit? How did Joseph exemplify this in his life?

_____

_____

_____

_____

_____

_____

How does having an *unusual spirit* position you to have a different approach to finances and prosperity? (Consider the example of Egypt during the years of plenty and season of famine.)

_____

_____

_____

_____

In what ways can practicing the *Joseph Principle* cause you to become an instrument of blessing and refreshing for others?

ACTION STEPS

Success always comes when preparation meets opportunity.
—HENRY HARTMAN

Think about how you can choose to have an excellent spirit. This is not something that people are naturally born with; it is a consistent and decisive choice. It is normal for people to crumble under their circumstances. As a result, many do not end up stepping into their destiny, enjoying the prosperous life that God has for them. God is willing; the problem is that we see opposition as fatal. Thus, it becomes so. If Joseph had this perspective, his dream would have died in the pit. But no. It survived the pit, Potiphar's house, and prison, ultimately bringing an entire nation into abundance. Never underestimate the power of having an excellent spirit. This is what positions you to experience the extraordinary—living beyond what is usual and ordinary!

Day Forty

THE LIFE THAT IS TRULY LIFE

*I came so they can have real and eternal life, more
and better life than they ever dreamed of.*
—JESUS
JOHN 10:10 MSG

I want today to be a day of evaluation, reflection, and contemplation for you. It should be a time of celebration. Congratulations! You are finished—and yet, just beginning! The goal for these resources has not been to simply provide you with more information. If that was the objective, writing another book could not compete with all of the other available options. No, the journey to *The Prosperous Soul* is not about reading a book or going through a devotional—it is about helping you see life differently. By now, I hope that you have a new definition of what prosperity looks like and have received some practical insight for how to experience it in your everyday life.

God is looking to prosper your whole being, not simply one facet. Perhaps you previously equated prosperity with financial gain. Maybe you considered prosperity something that good Christians should *not* get wrapped up in because of the abuses or misuses you have heard about or even experienced firsthand. The goal of this study is to help you catch a fresh glimpse of prosperity in its truest sense.

I humbly invite you to use today as a time to consider *how* you think about prosperity now. How you define prosperity will determine *what* you pursue. If you think prosperity is just "cash in the bank" or the acquisition of material wealth, then your pursuit will be misguided. When asked to describe prosperity, megachurch pastor and best-selling author Joel Osteen described it this way, "The way I define prosperity is that I believe God wants you to prosper in your health, in your family, in your relationships, in your business, and in your career."[1]

At this point, I suspect and pray that you have read through *The Prosperous Soul* book and are one day away from completing this devotional journey. The format for today's entry flows differently from the others. My goal over these past forty days has been to help you redefine what a *rich life* really looks like. I want to walk with you through this reflection process, help you to identify the conclusions you have come to, and lead you to take the next step in the journey.

REFLECTION QUESTIONS

How do you understand prosperity differently after you have completed this journey?

Prosperity does *not* end with you. Even if you have a broader definition of the concept but, ultimately, are pursuing it with a selfish final end, you are missing the point. Wholeness must be shared. People need to see you prospering in areas where they are experiencing opposition, lack, and difficulty so they can be drawn into hope. Your prosperity gives other people hope that they can experience the same kind of wholeness.

This is the key purpose of prosperity. Not only are you introducing people to the abundant life that is available, but you are also pointing them to the Life Giver. Wholeness is a direct result of your relationship with the God of Wholeness. He is the One who enables you to walk in the "*life that is truly life*" (1 Tim. 6:19 NIV).

How can the world become a better place when you walk in wholeness and prosperity?

_____

_____

_____

_____

_____

ACTION STEPS

Where there is no vision, the people perish.
—PROVERBS 29:18 KJV

Between *The Prosperous Soul* book and devotional, we have 1) defined what true prosperity is, and 2) discovered forty key practices to living a richer life.

Perhaps you are now asking, "*How do I sustain prosperity in my soul?*" In other words, how do you ensure that this journey was not just a book or devotional, but a new way of approaching life?

Vision

If you have a clear vision for what the prosperous soul and richer life looks like, then your progress will be sustained. Without vision, people give up and progress perishes.

I encourage you to periodically review the 40 prosperity practices listed in this devotional and in the book. Start to implement them into your everyday life. Don't overwhelm yourself. Although there are 40 practices, you are not expected to implement all of them at once. Focus on one each week and make *The Prosperous Soul* study a year-long personal development project. Don't make it a burden. These practices are specifically designed to bring you into new levels of freedom and blessing in *every* area of your life!

1.   Michelle A. Vu, "Joel Osteen on Prosperity Gospel, Crystal Cathedral, and Jesus," The Christian Post, April 29, 2012, http://www.christianpost.com/news/interview-joel-osteen-on-prosperity-gospel-crystal-cathedral-and-jesus-74040.

ABOUT DR. N. CINDY TRIMM

*A*s a best-selling author, keynote speaker, and former senator of Bermuda, Dr. Trimm is a sought-after empowerment specialist, thought leader, and advocate for cultural change. Listed among *Ebony* magazine's *Power 100* as the "top 100 doers and influencers in the world today," Dr. Trimm consults with civic, nonprofit, and religious leaders around the world. With a background in government, education, theology, and human development, Dr. Trimm translates powerful spiritual truth into everyday language that empowers individuals to transform their lives and their communities.

Trimm International is a pioneering force in the personal and leadership development field. On the forefront of transforming culture through empowering individuals to lead change, Trimm International provides cutting-edge programs and innovative products that inspire, equip, and empower people to impact their world.

CindyTrimm.com
Let's stay connected!

CINDY TRIMM

Be sure to visit us online at *CindyTrimm.com* for lots of online resources to empower, equip and encourage you daily!

Videos • Blogs • Articles
Speaking Event Schedule • TV Broadcast Information
Online Resources • Email Subscribe
...and more!

 @cindytrimm

 facebook.com/drtimm